This book belongs to.....

....

....

Small preview of what's inside

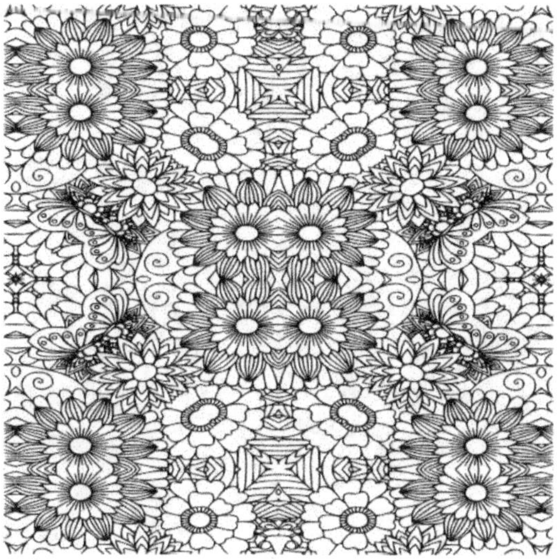
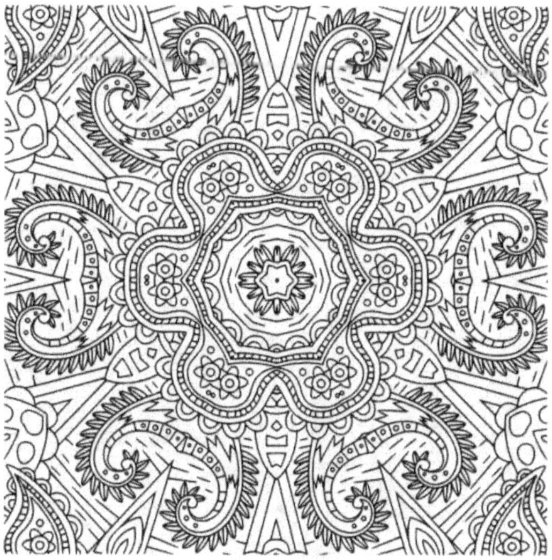
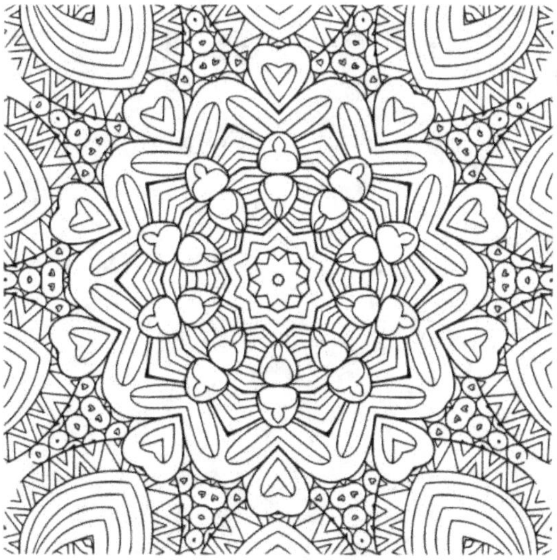
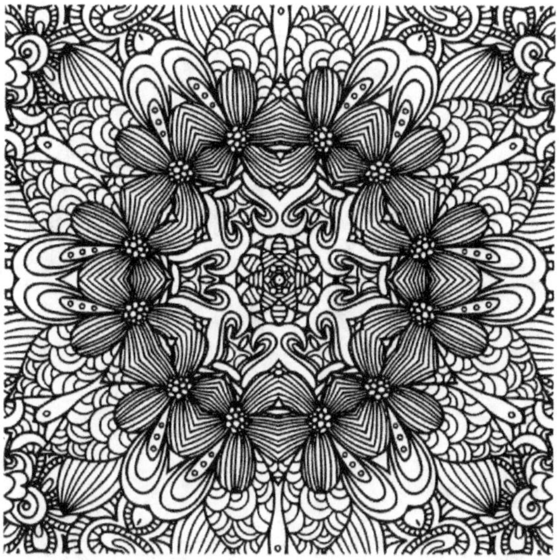
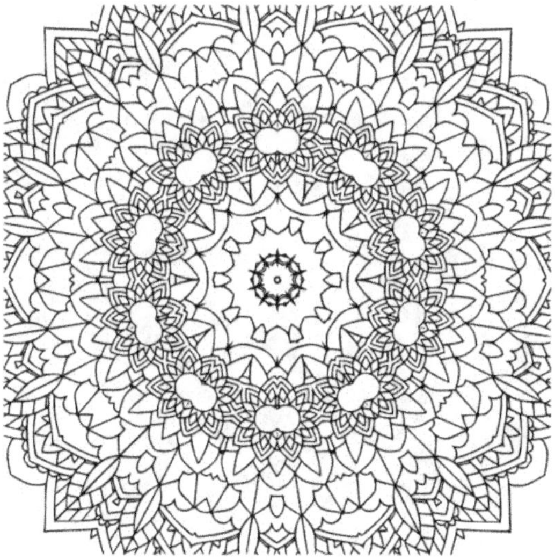
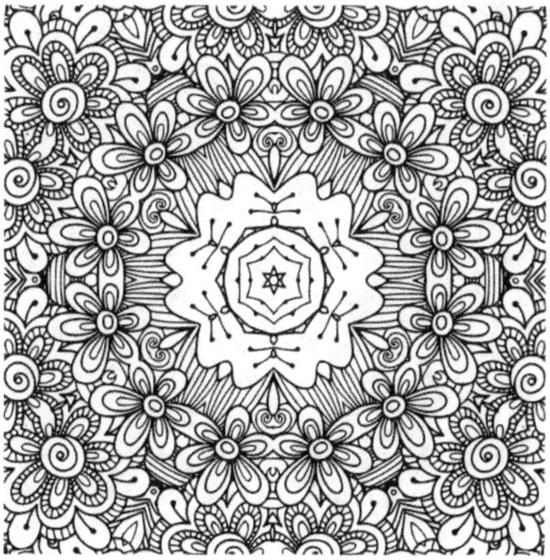

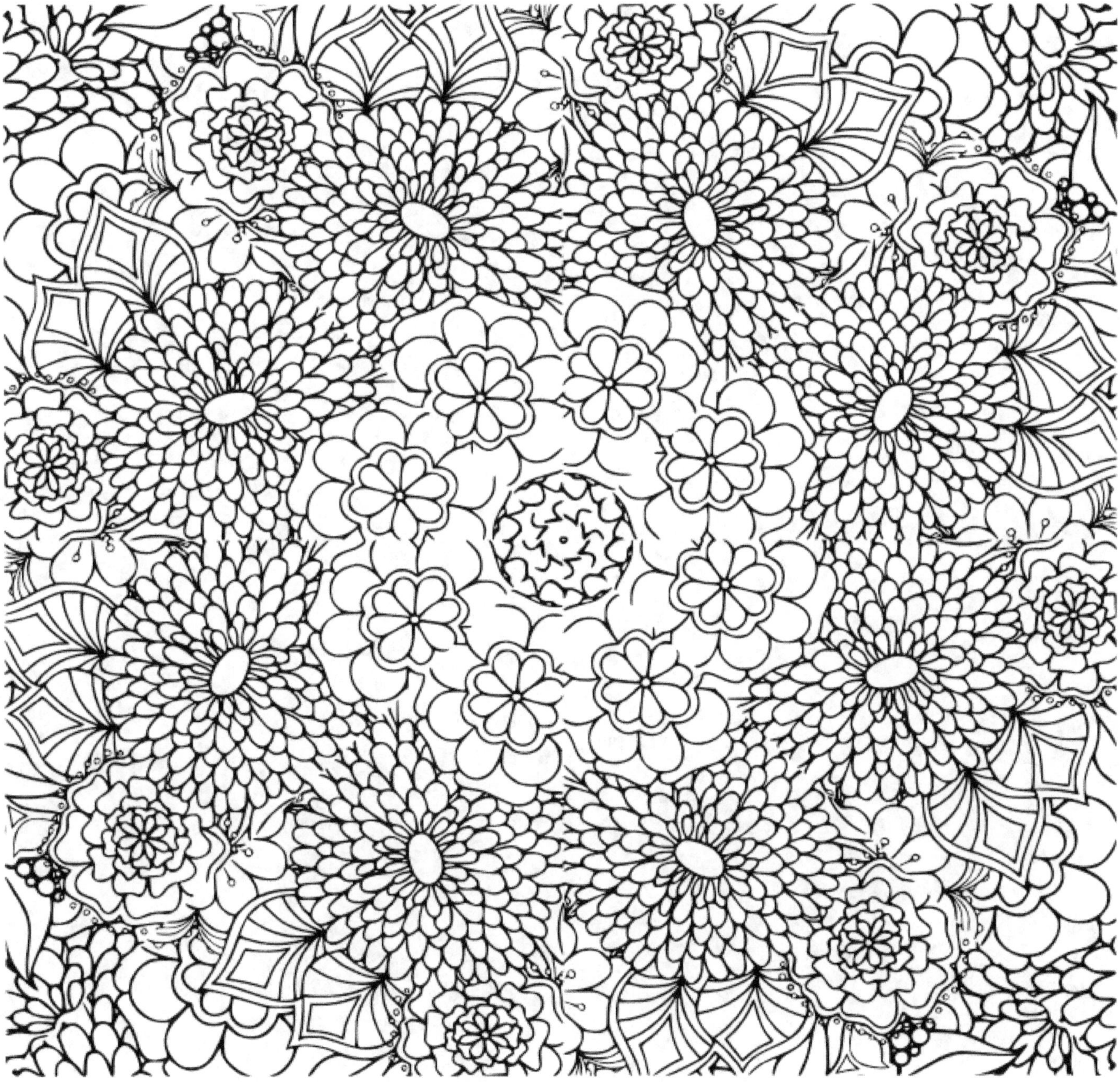

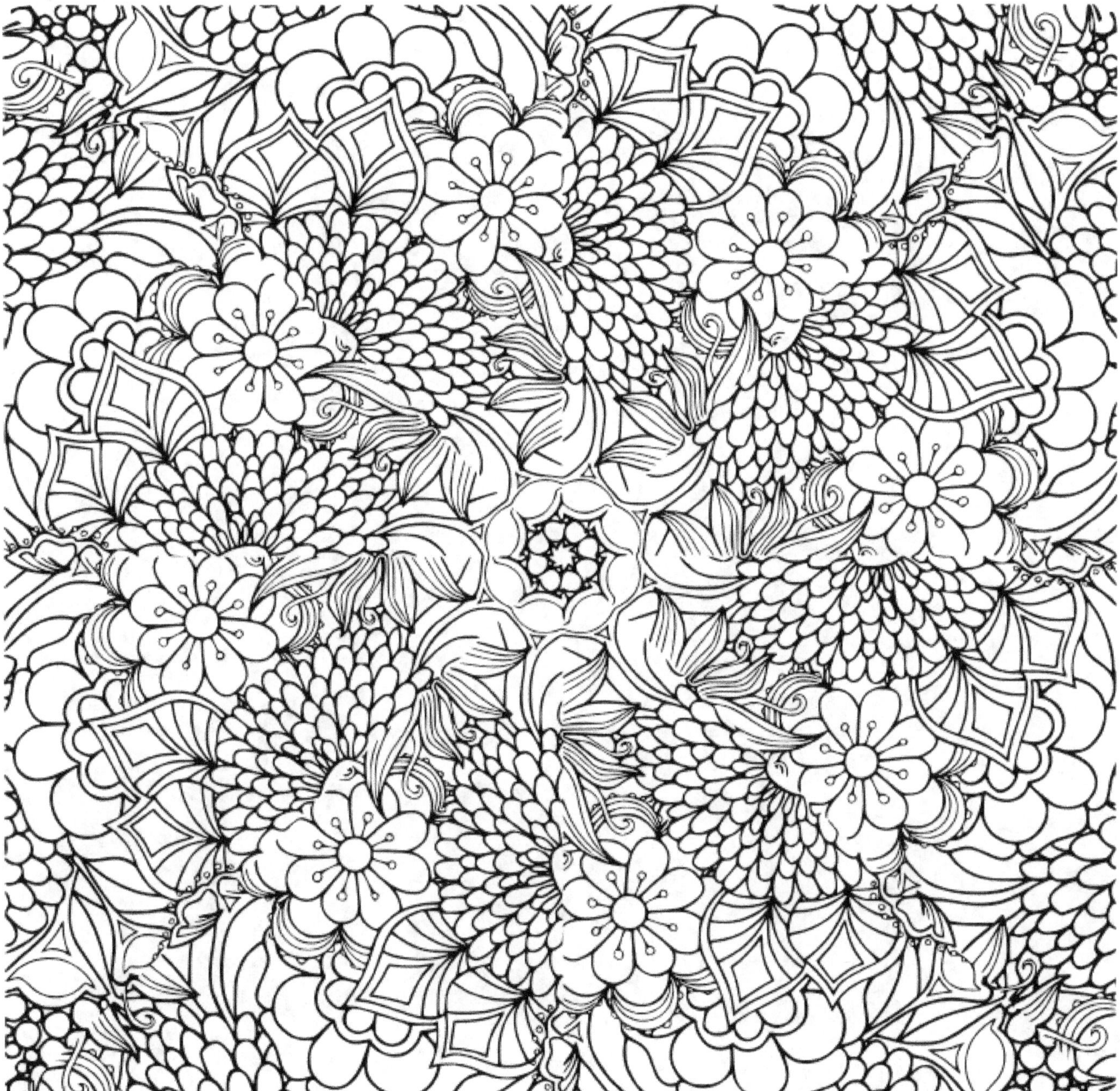

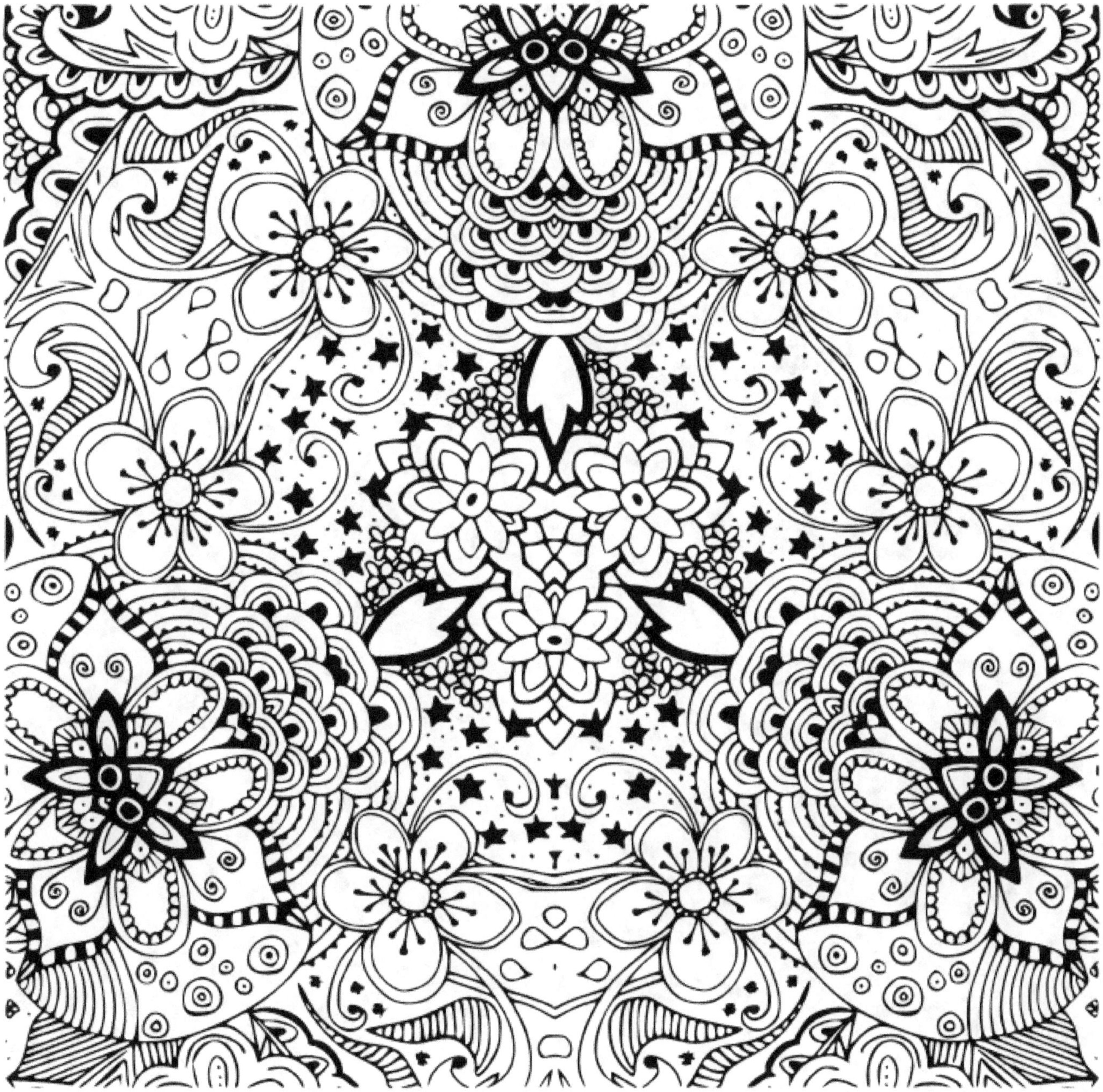

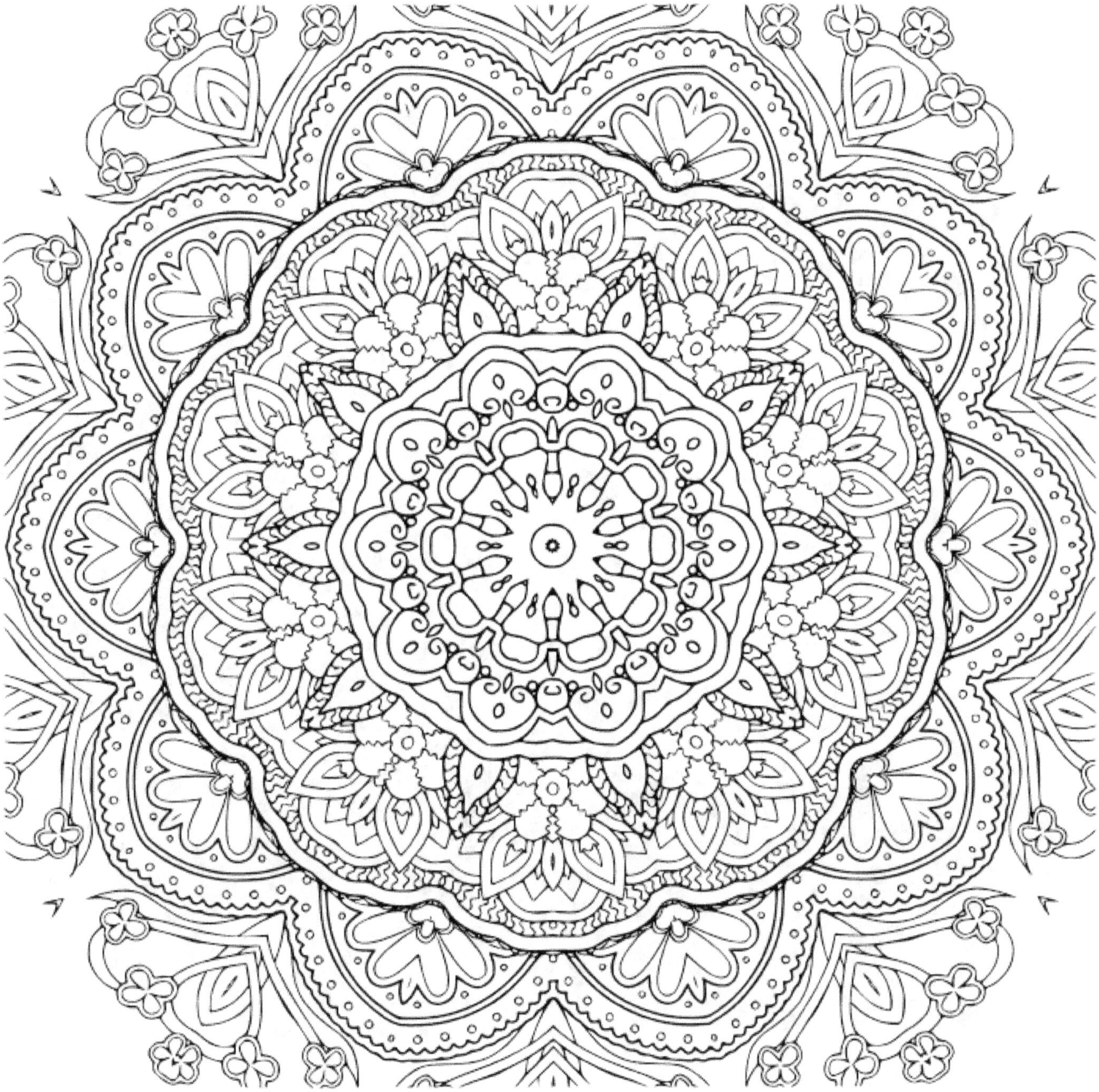

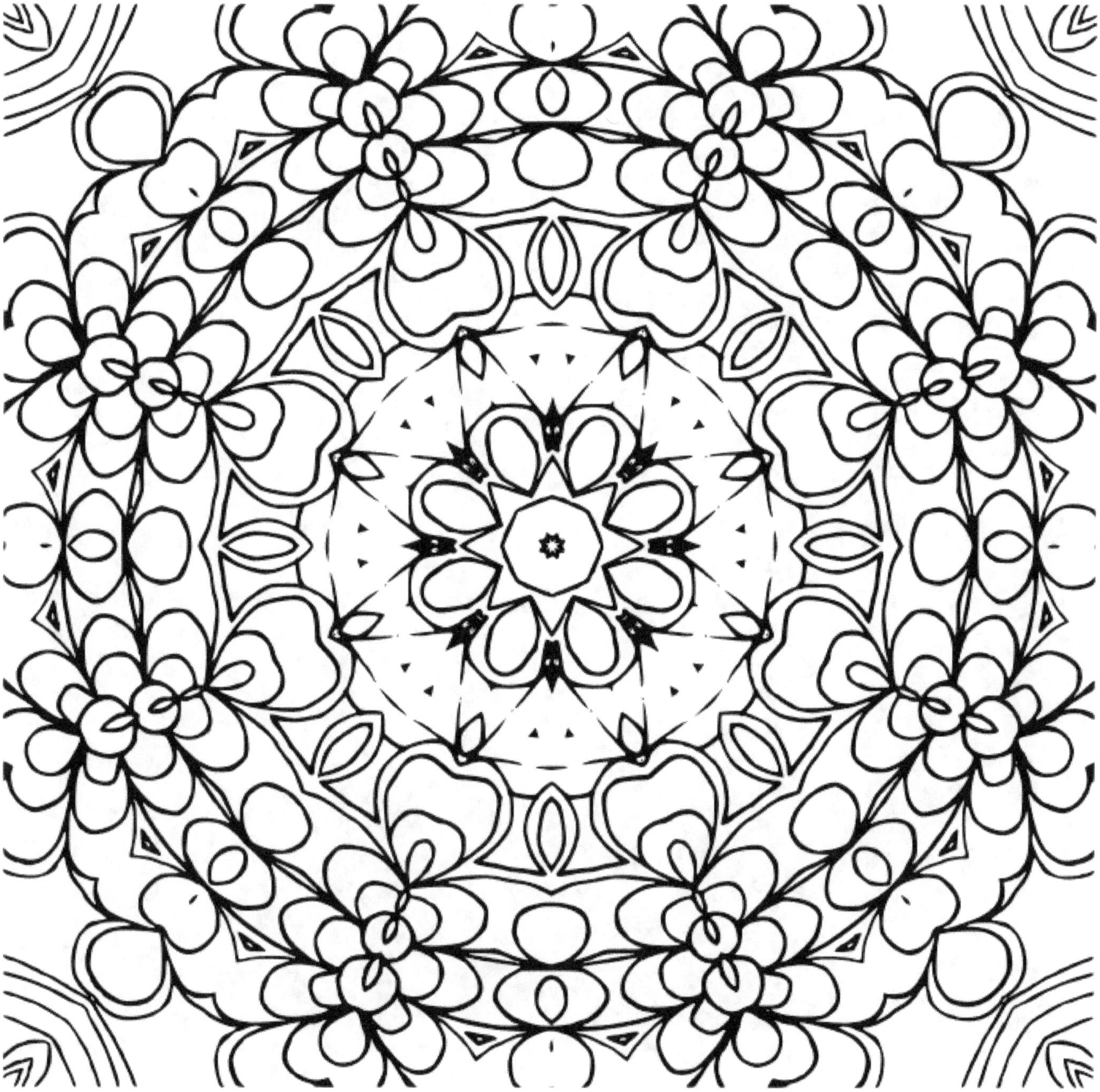

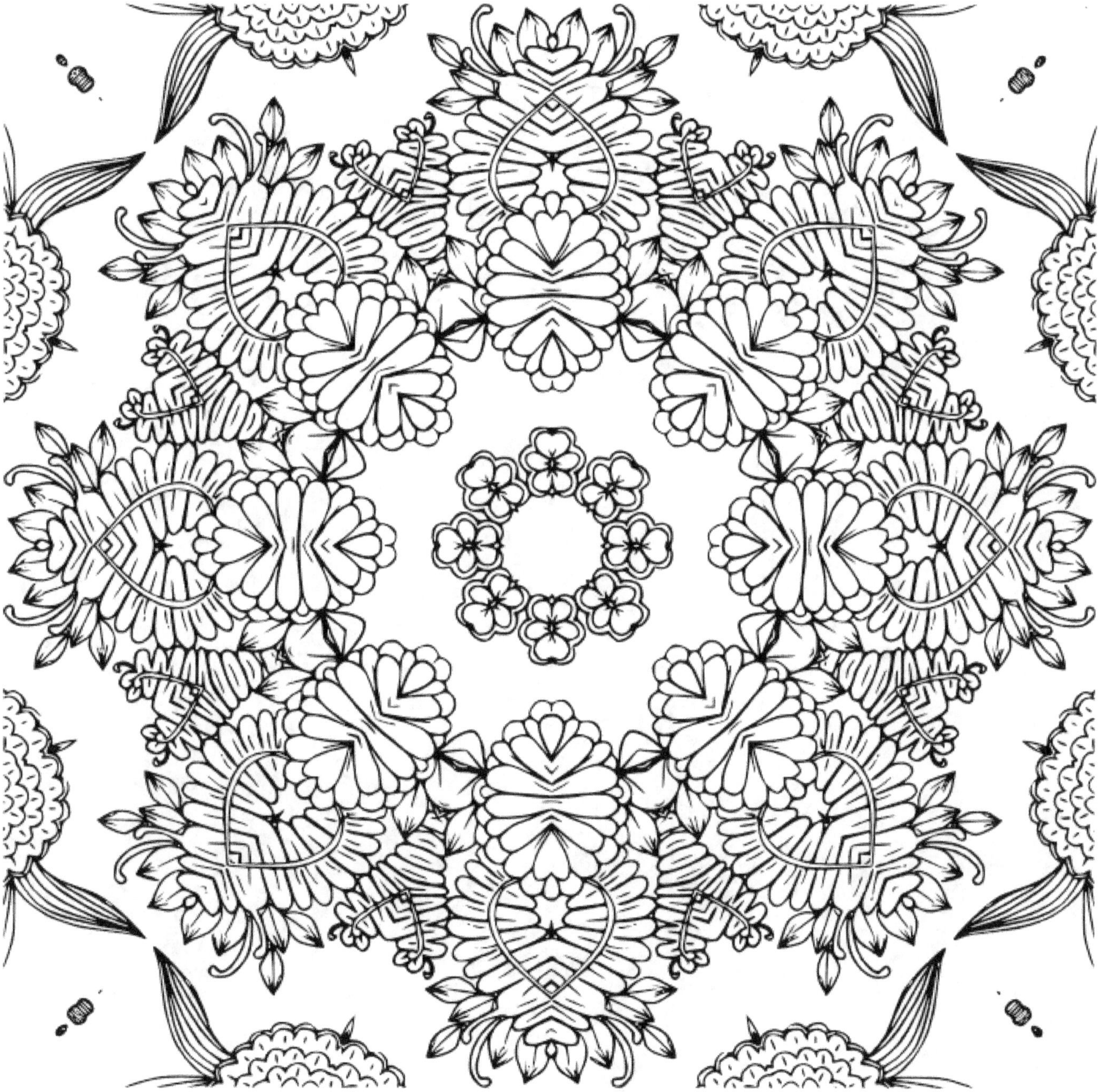

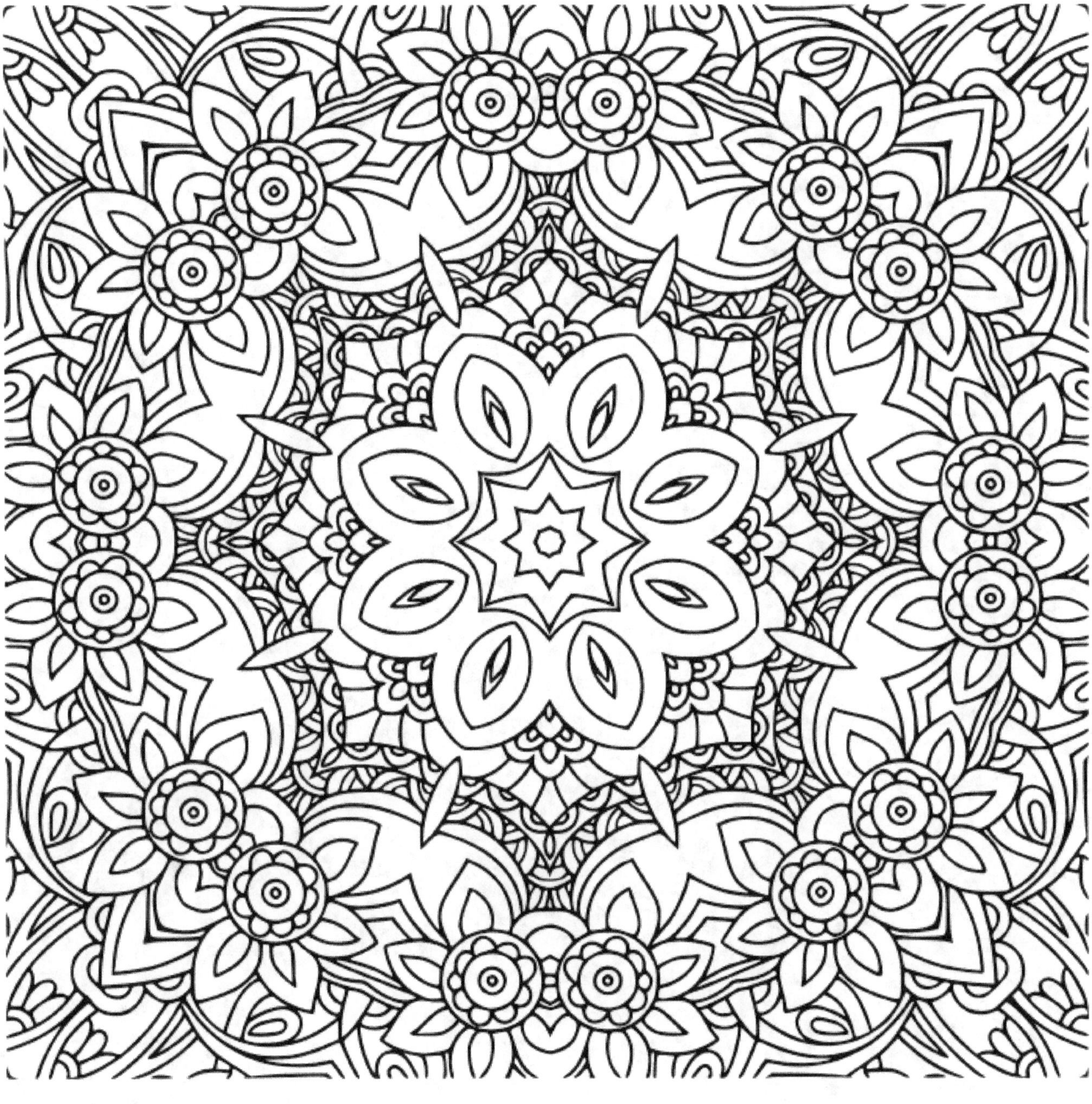

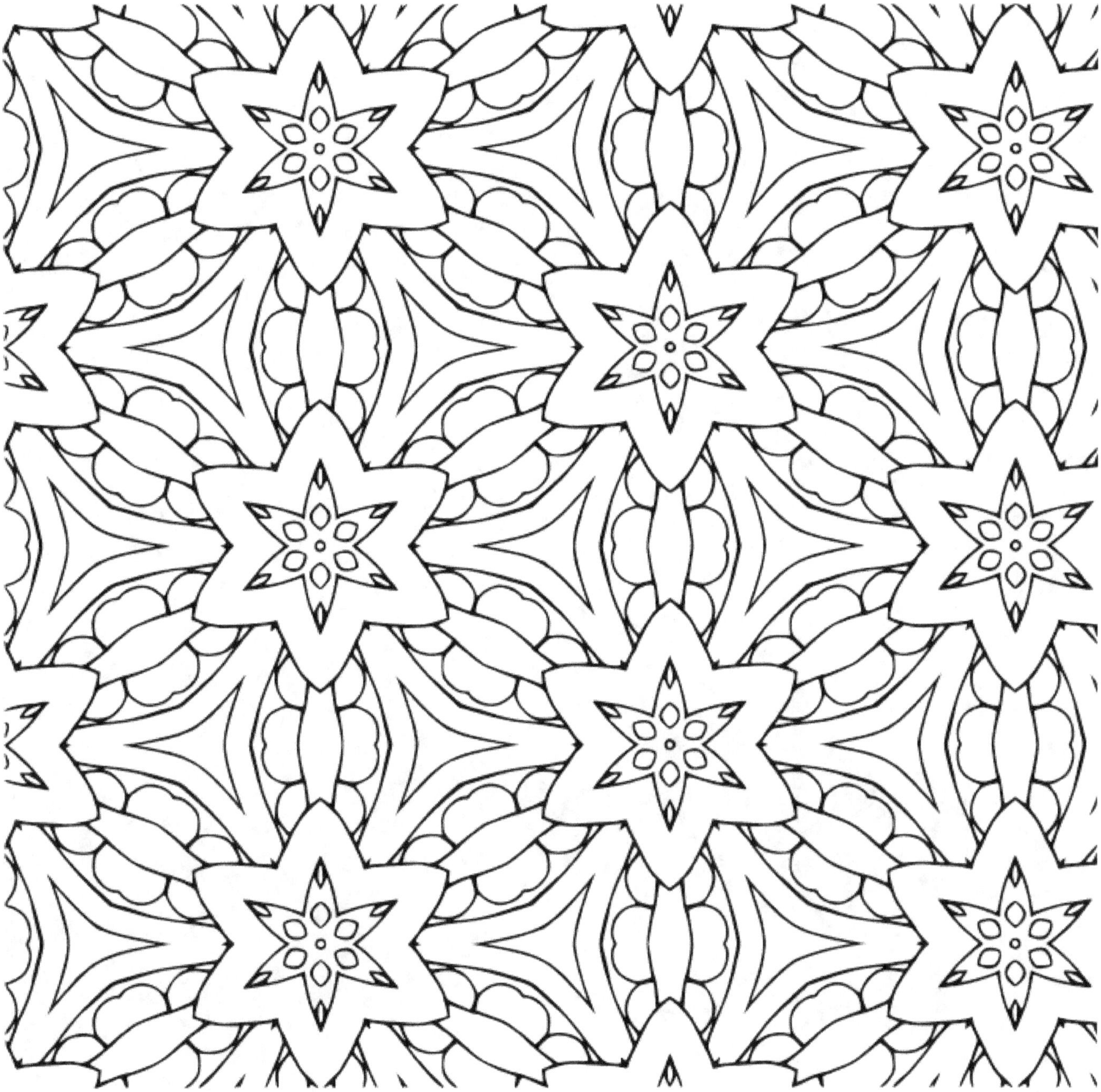

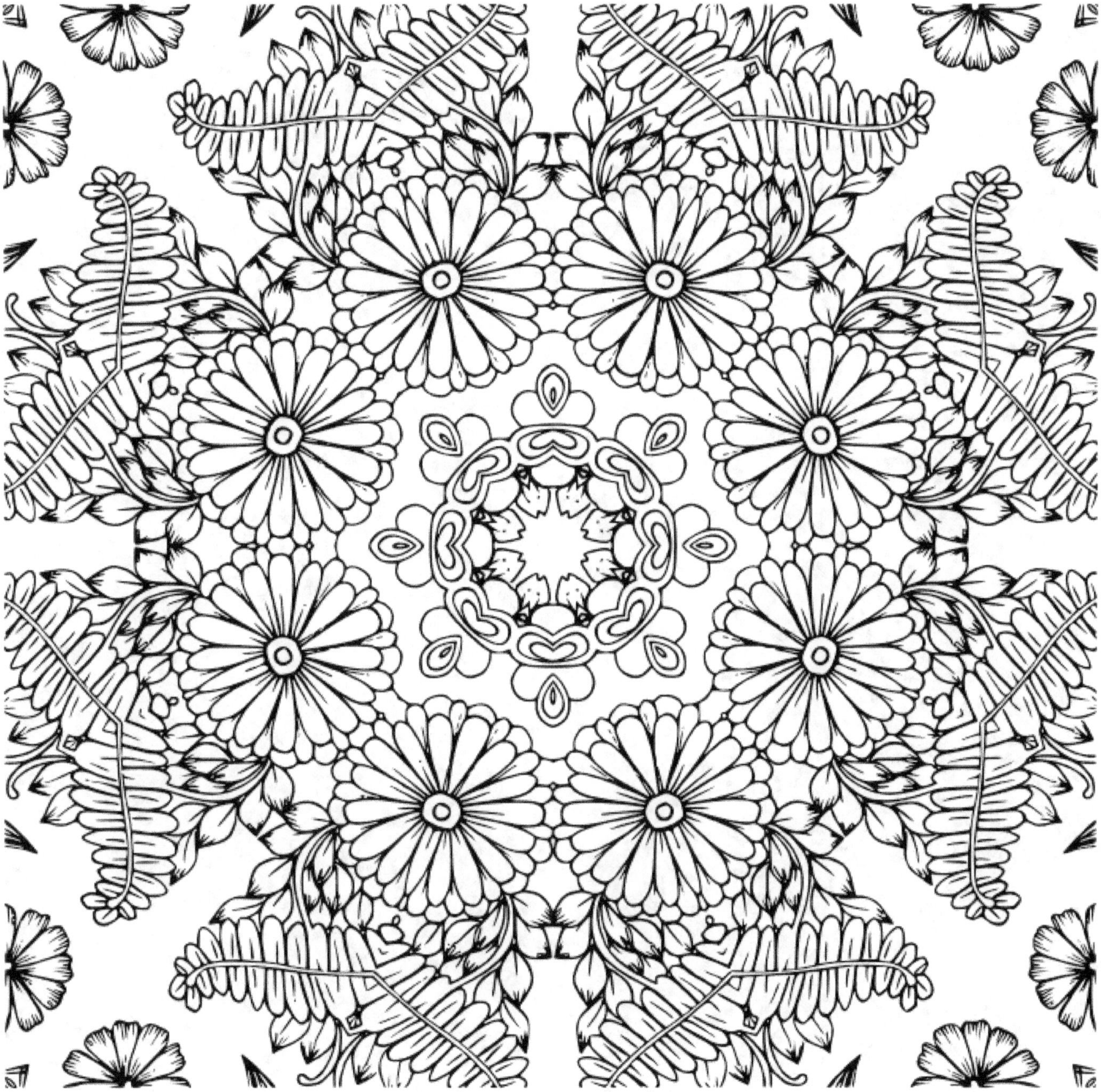

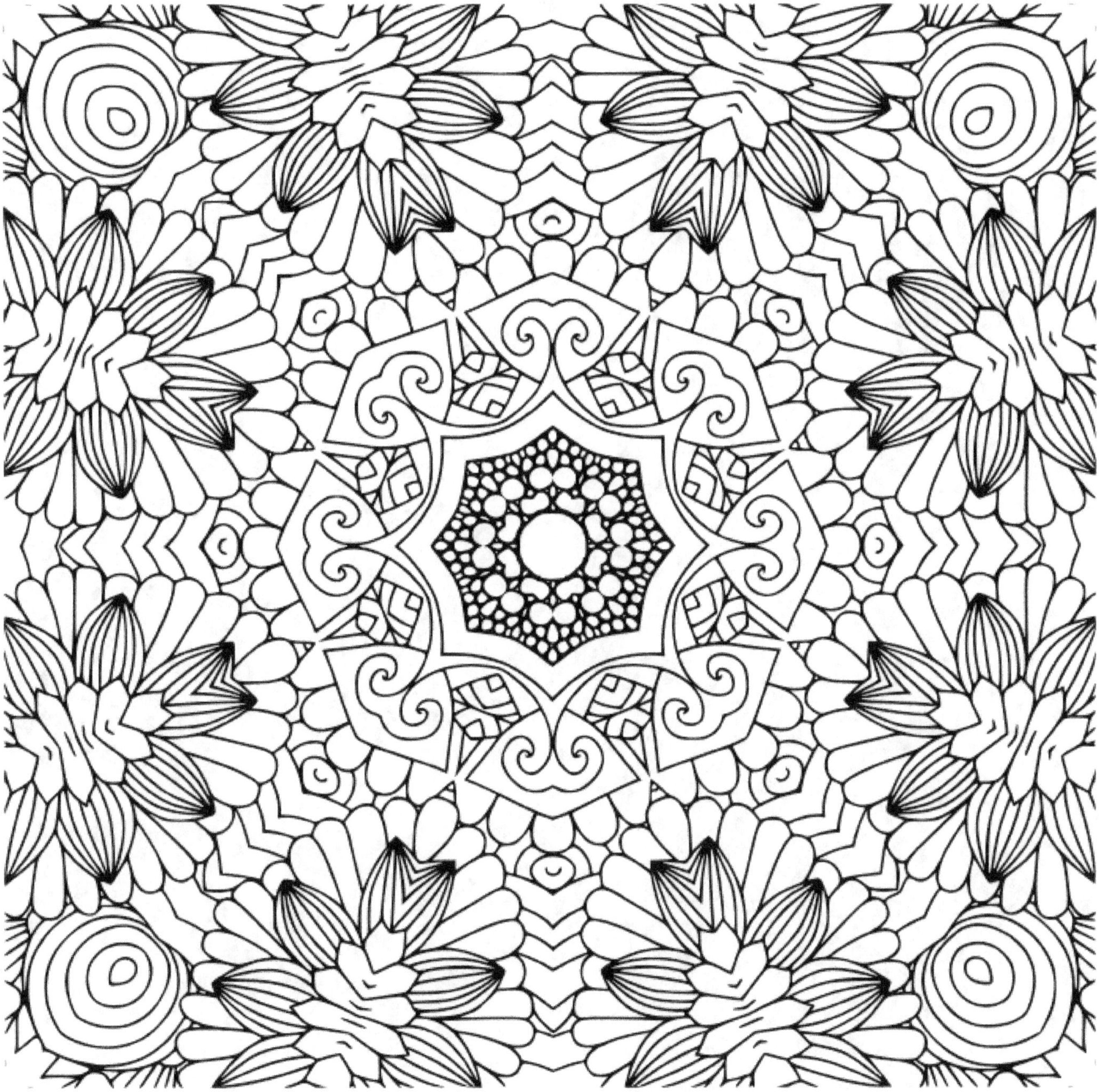

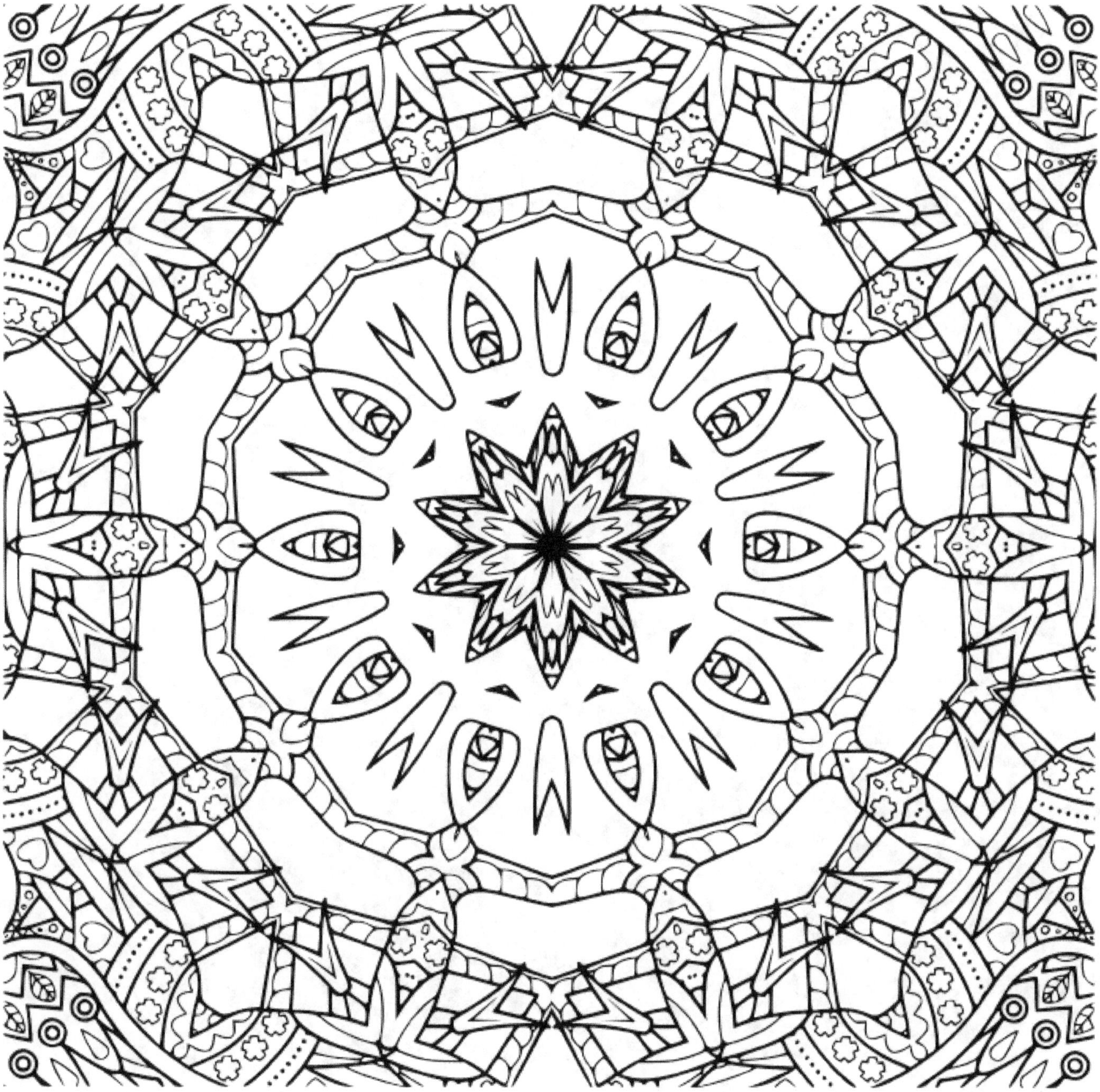

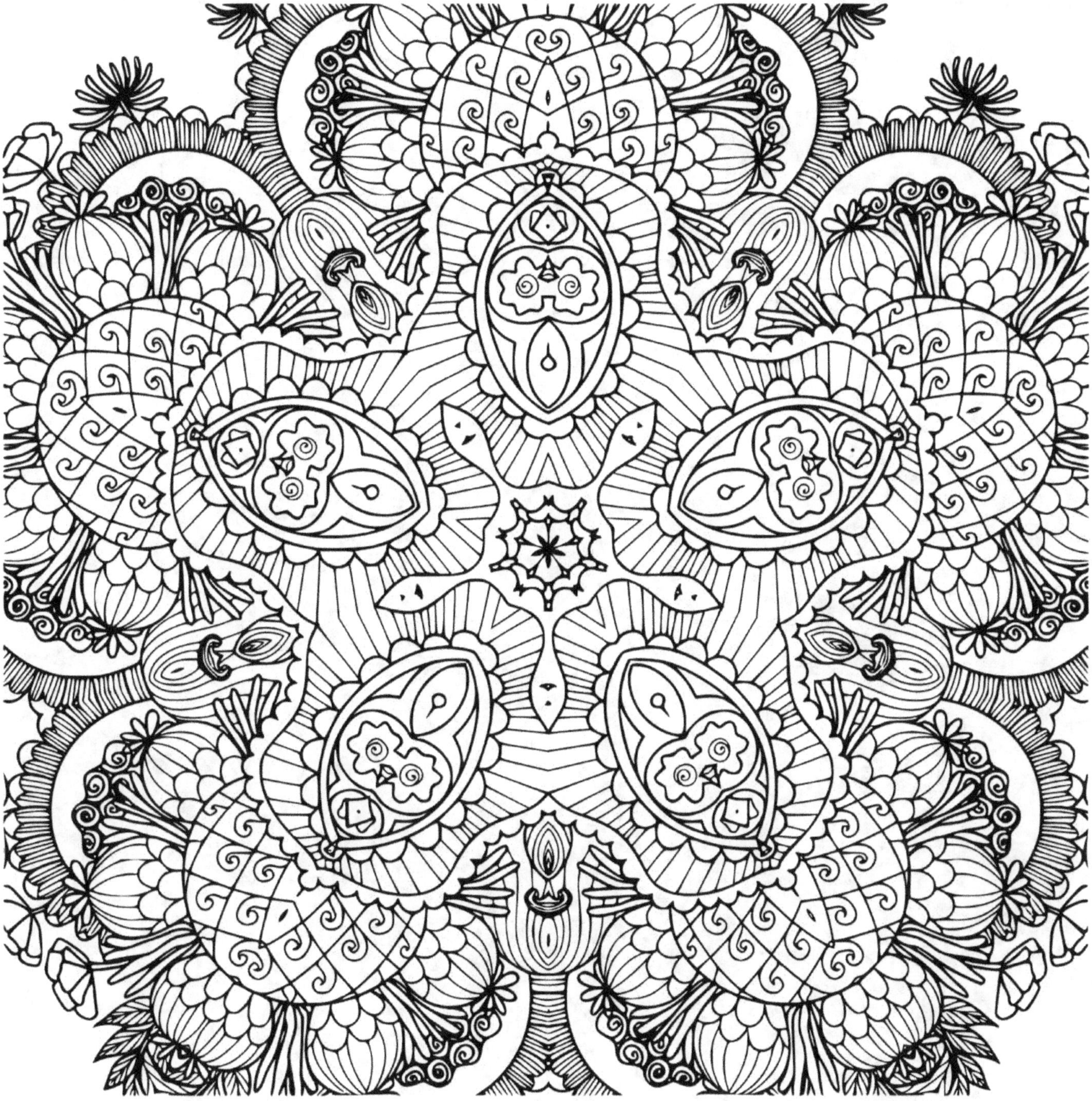

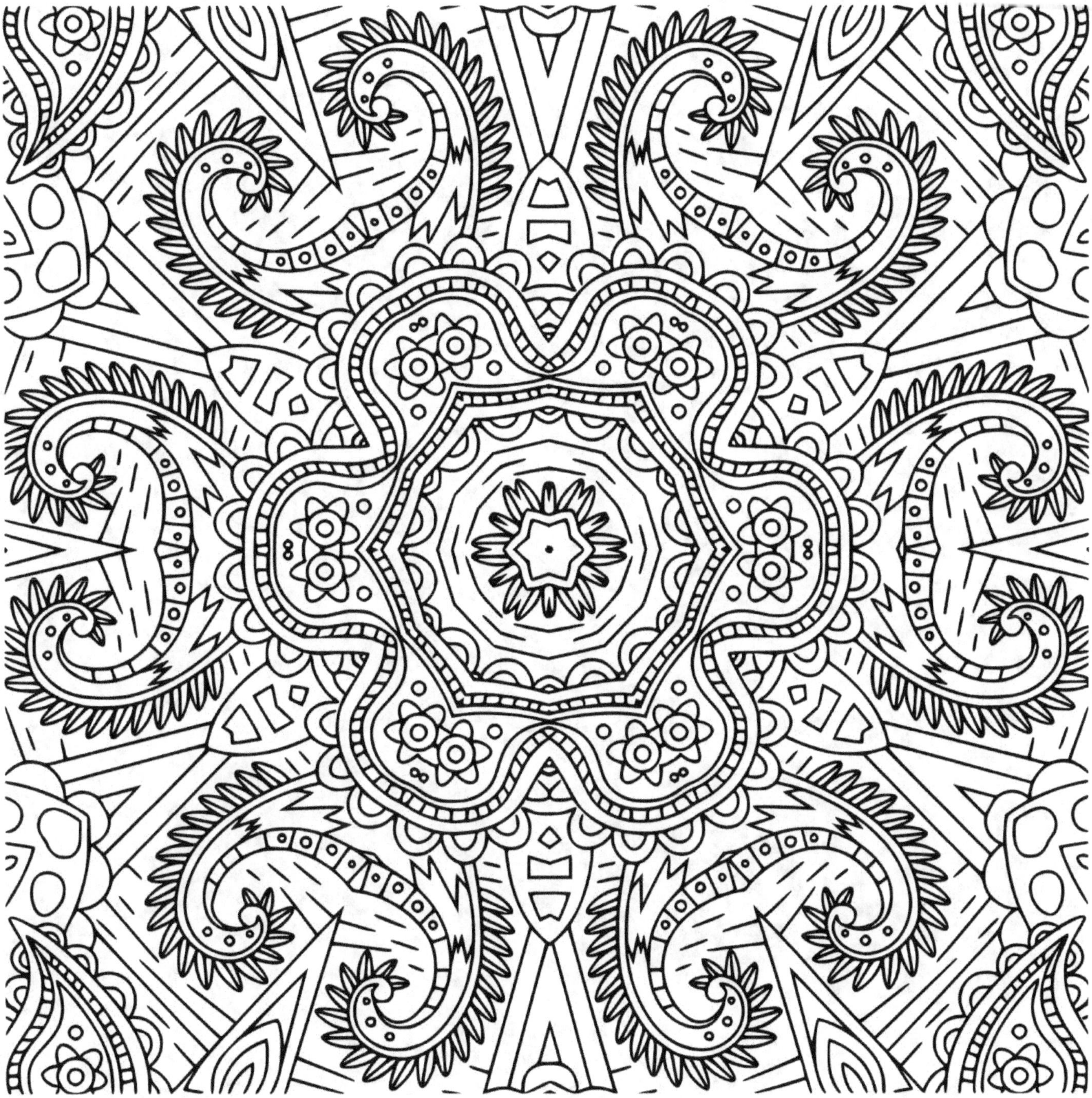

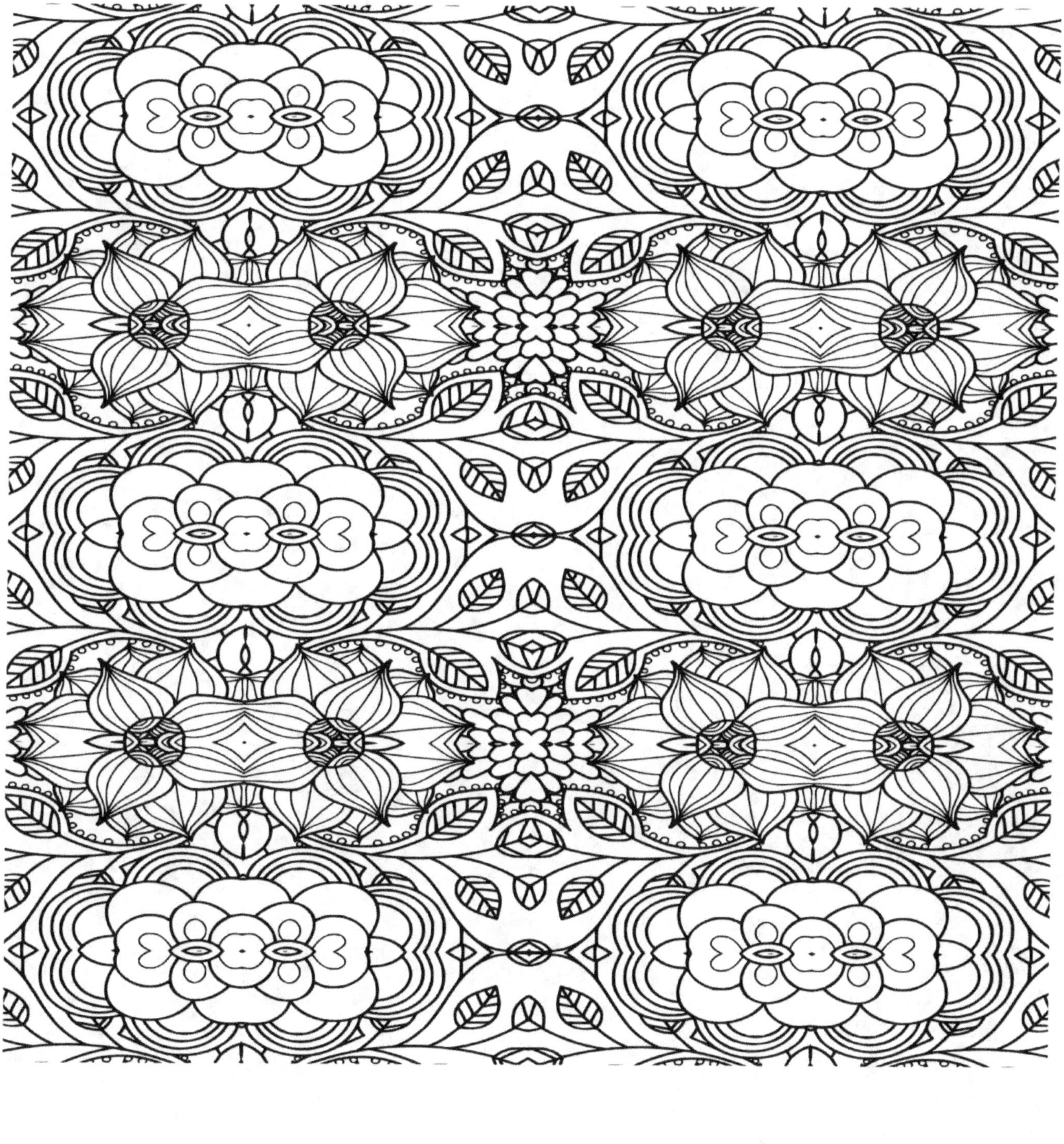

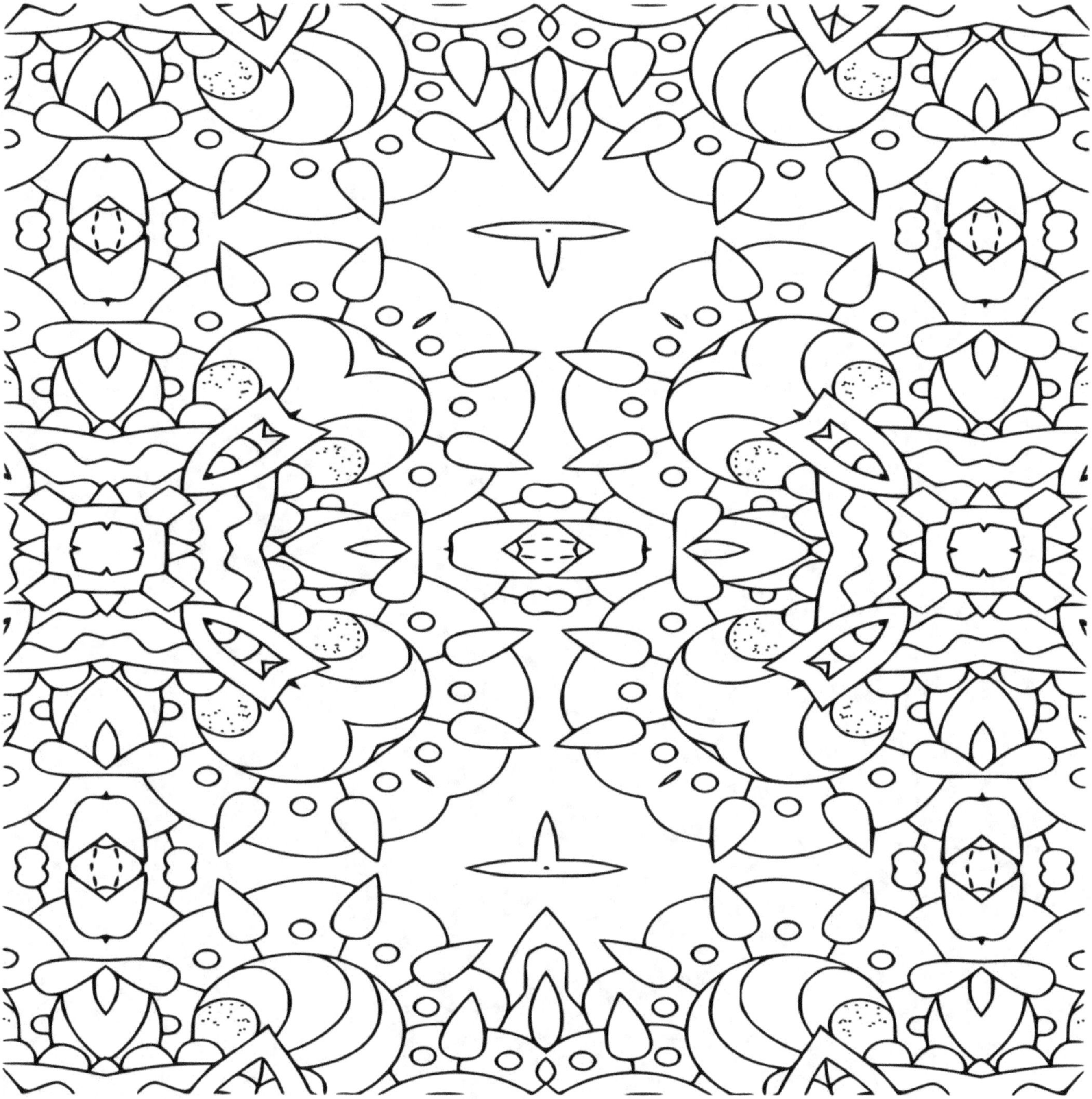

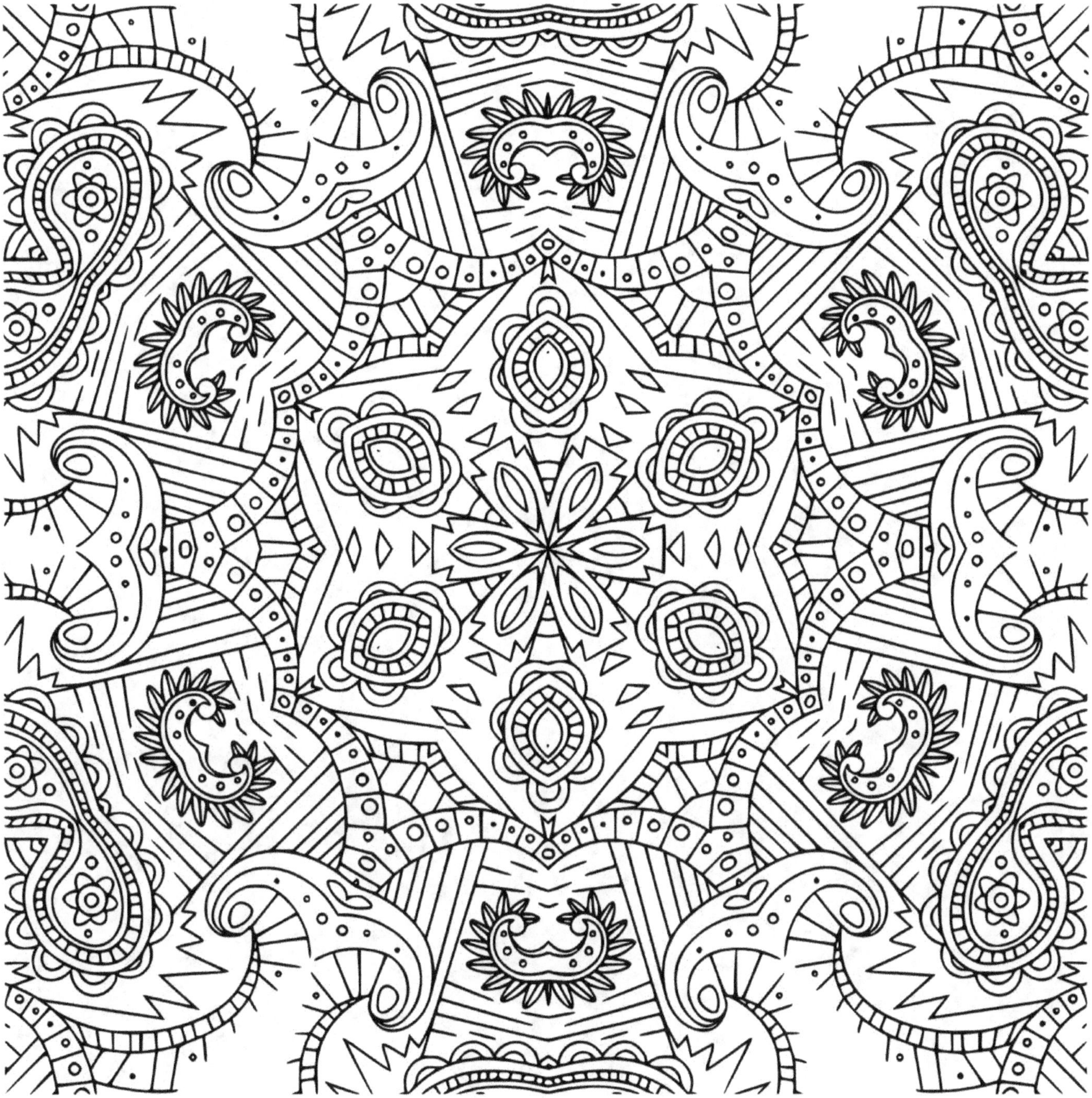

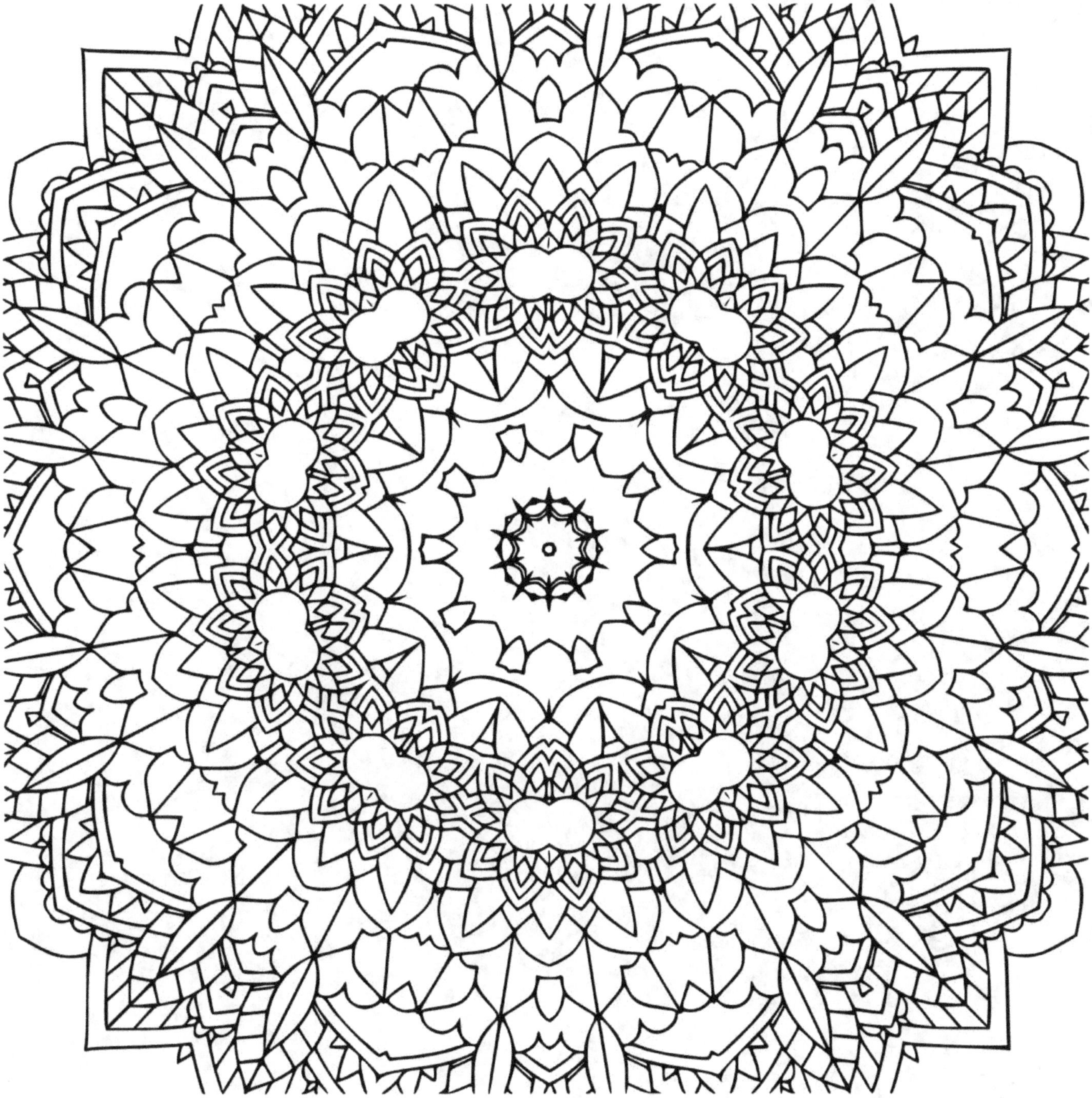

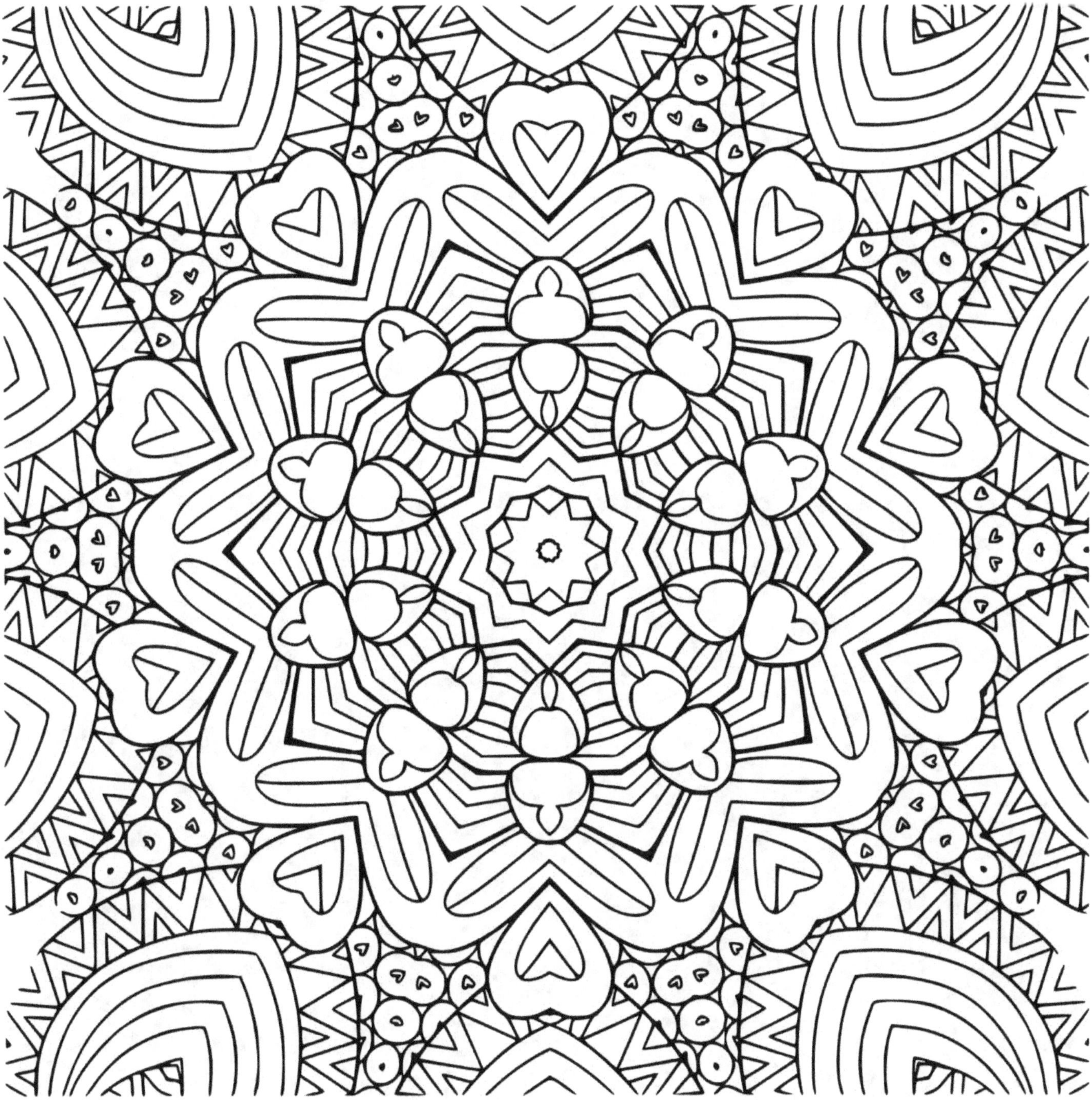

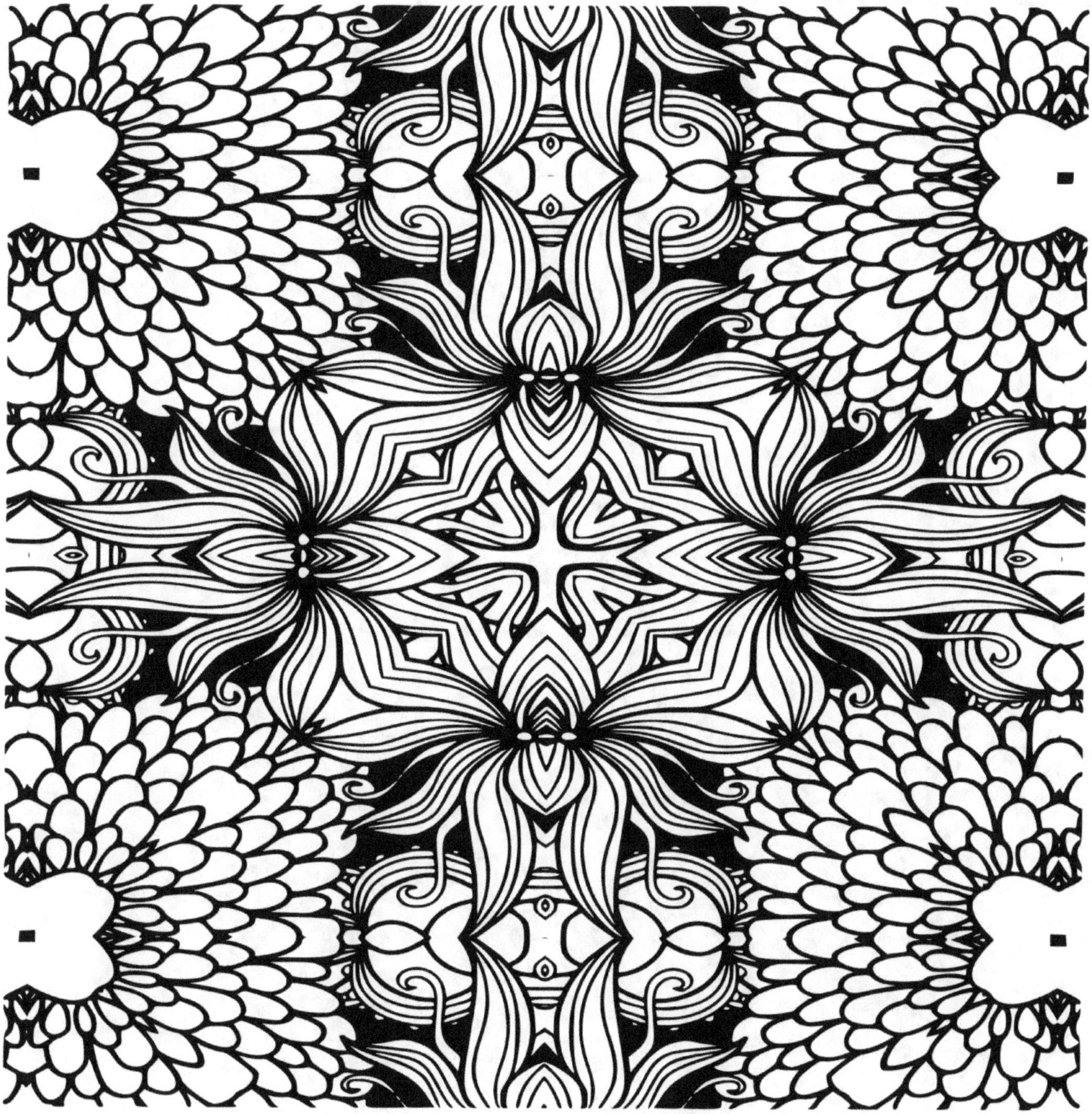

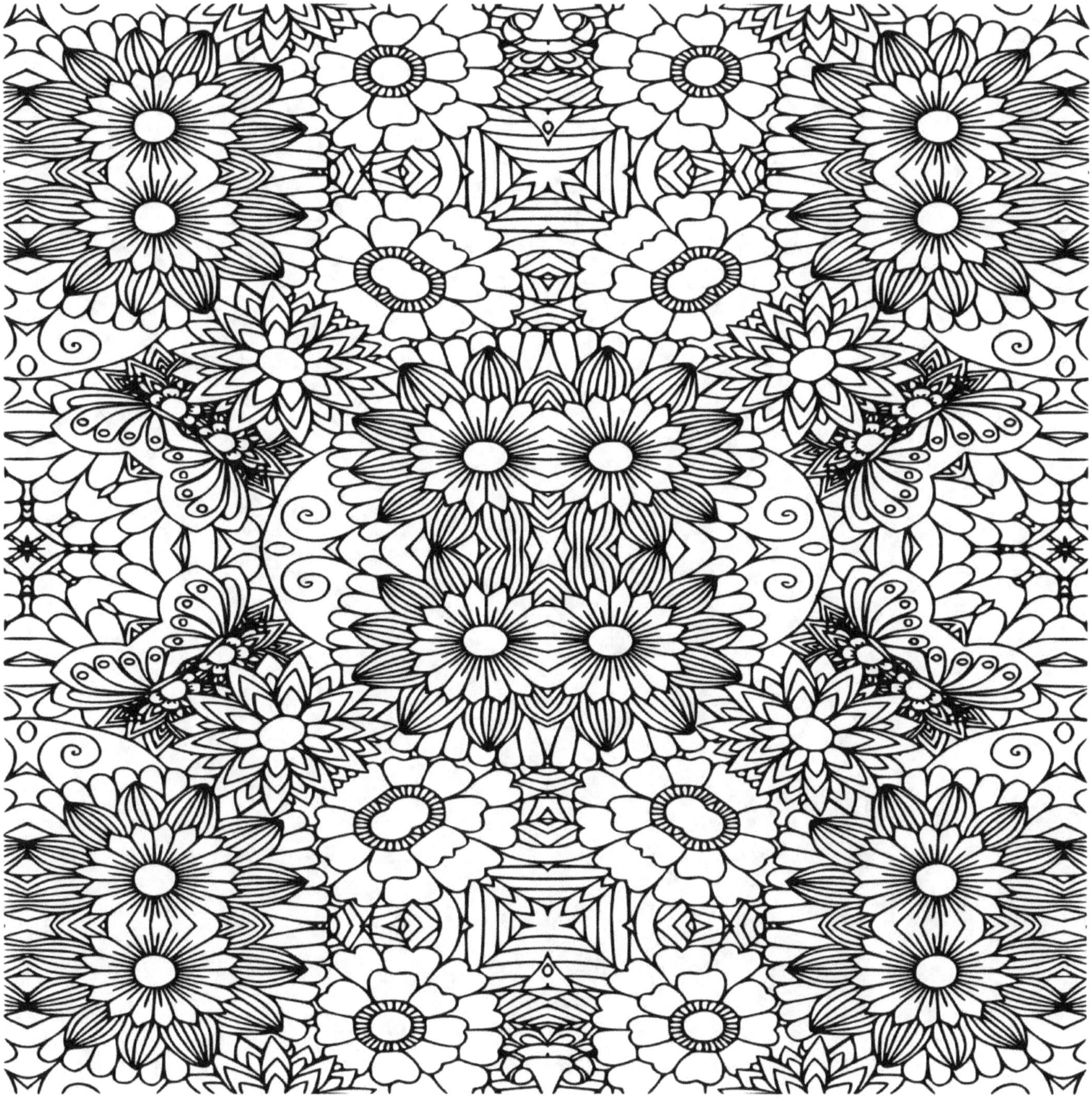

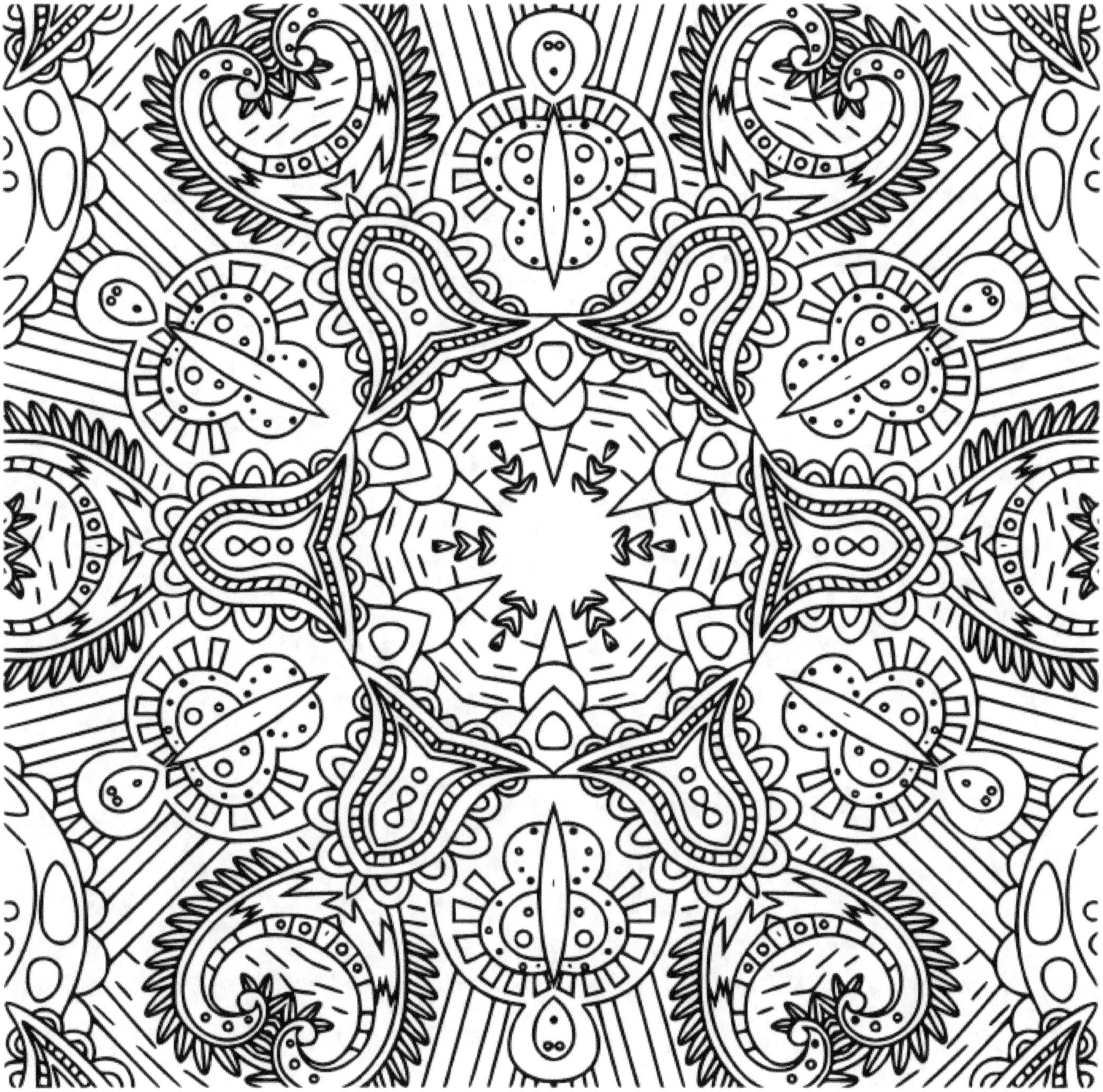

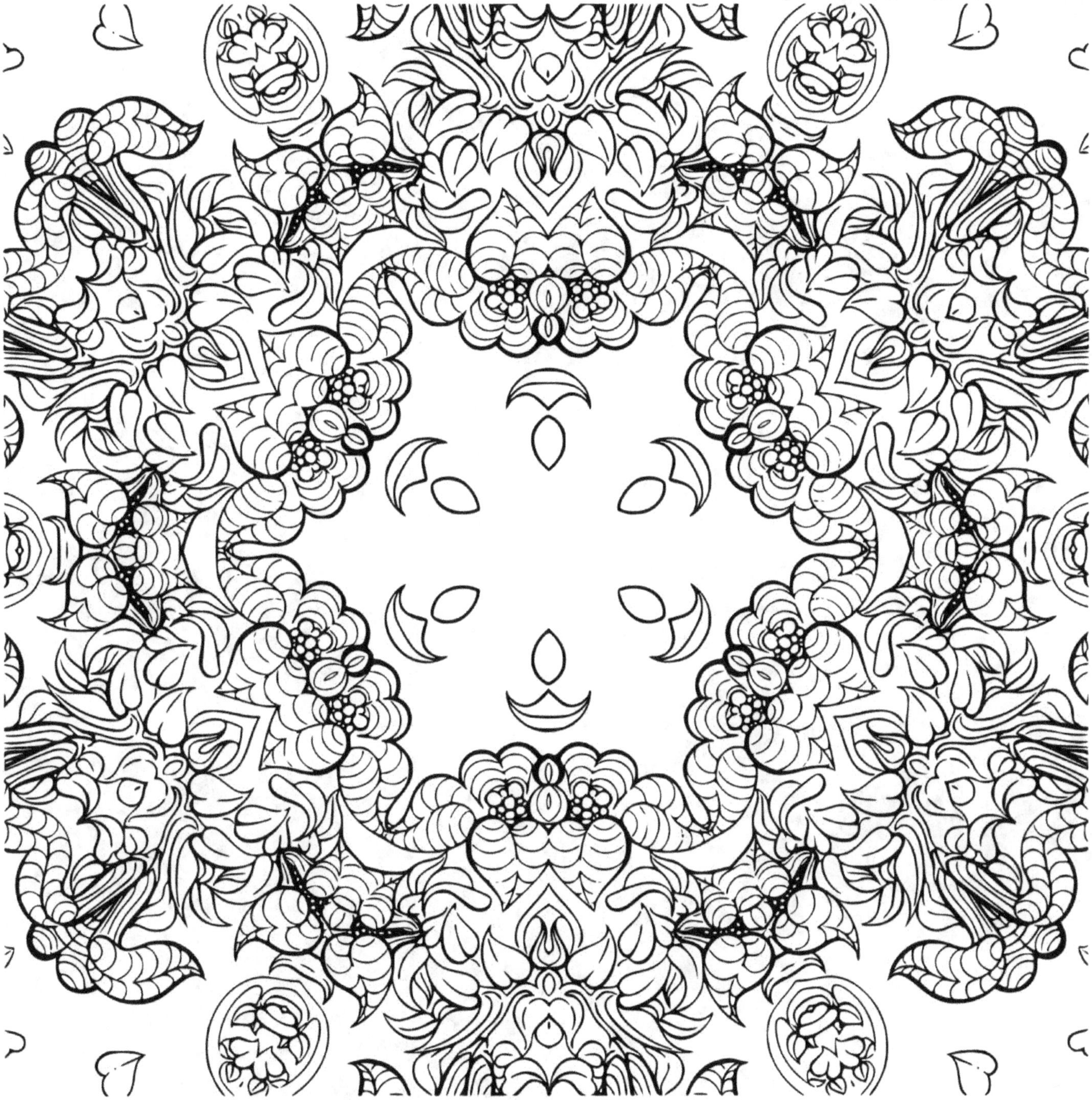

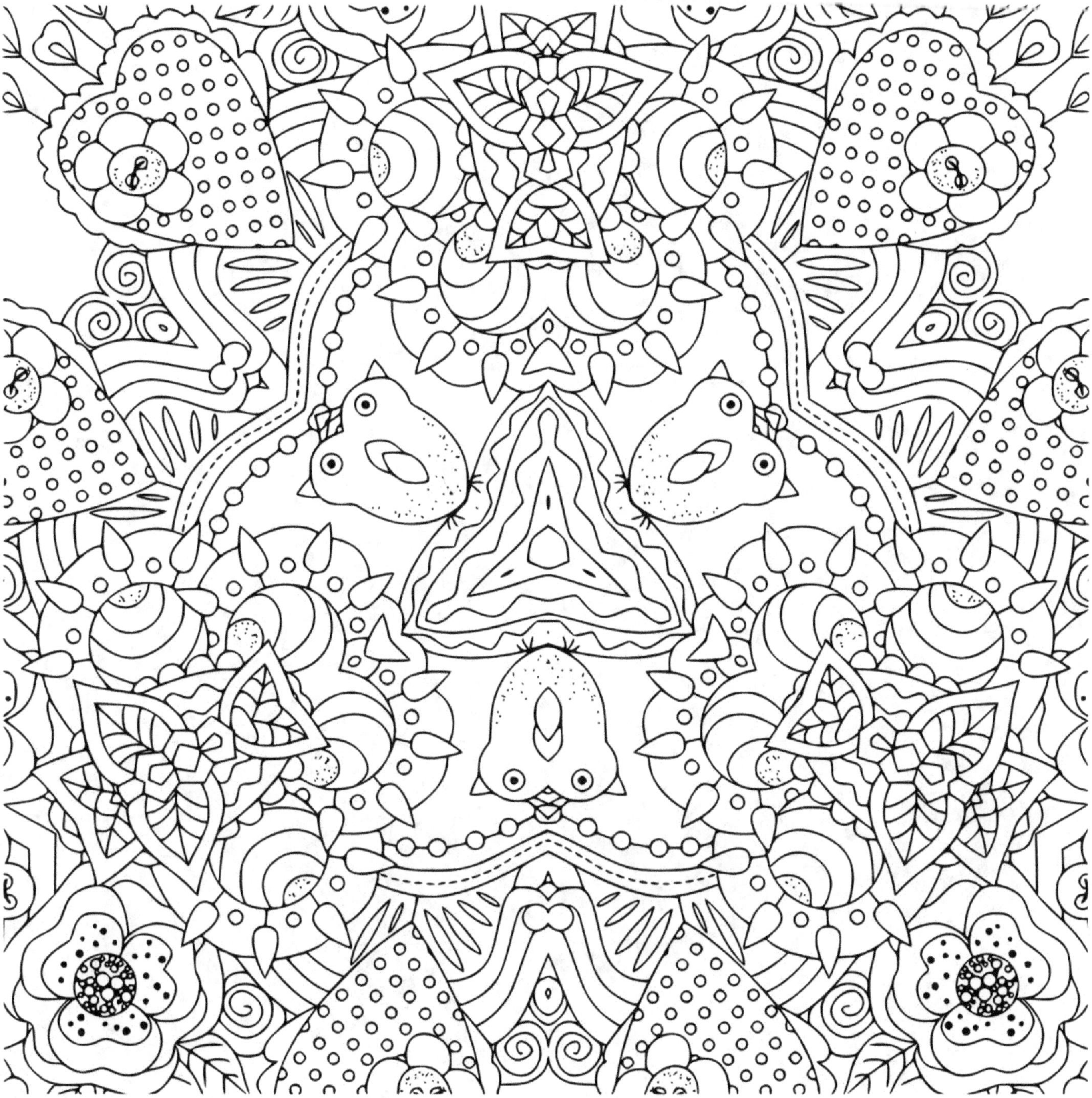

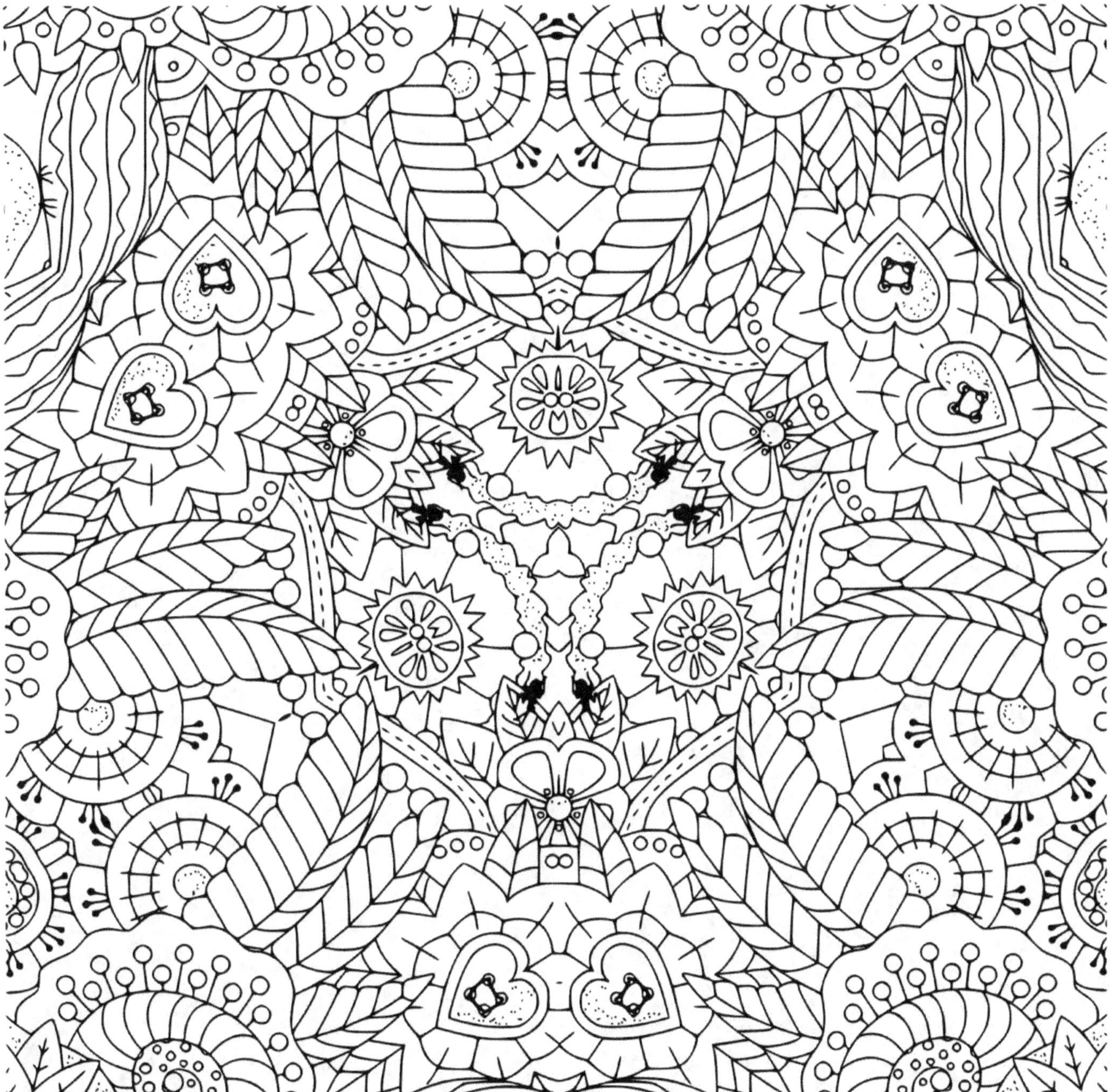

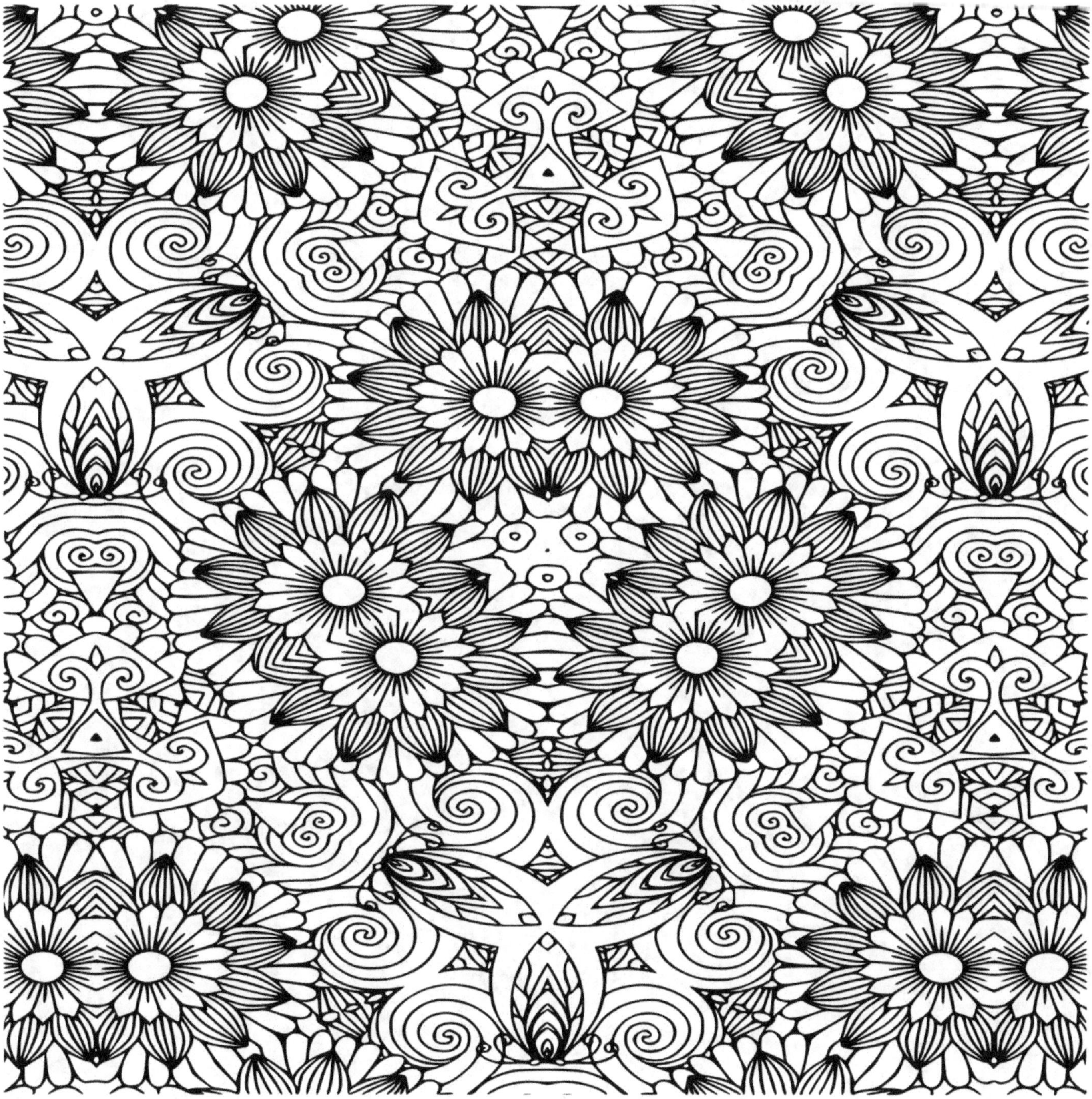

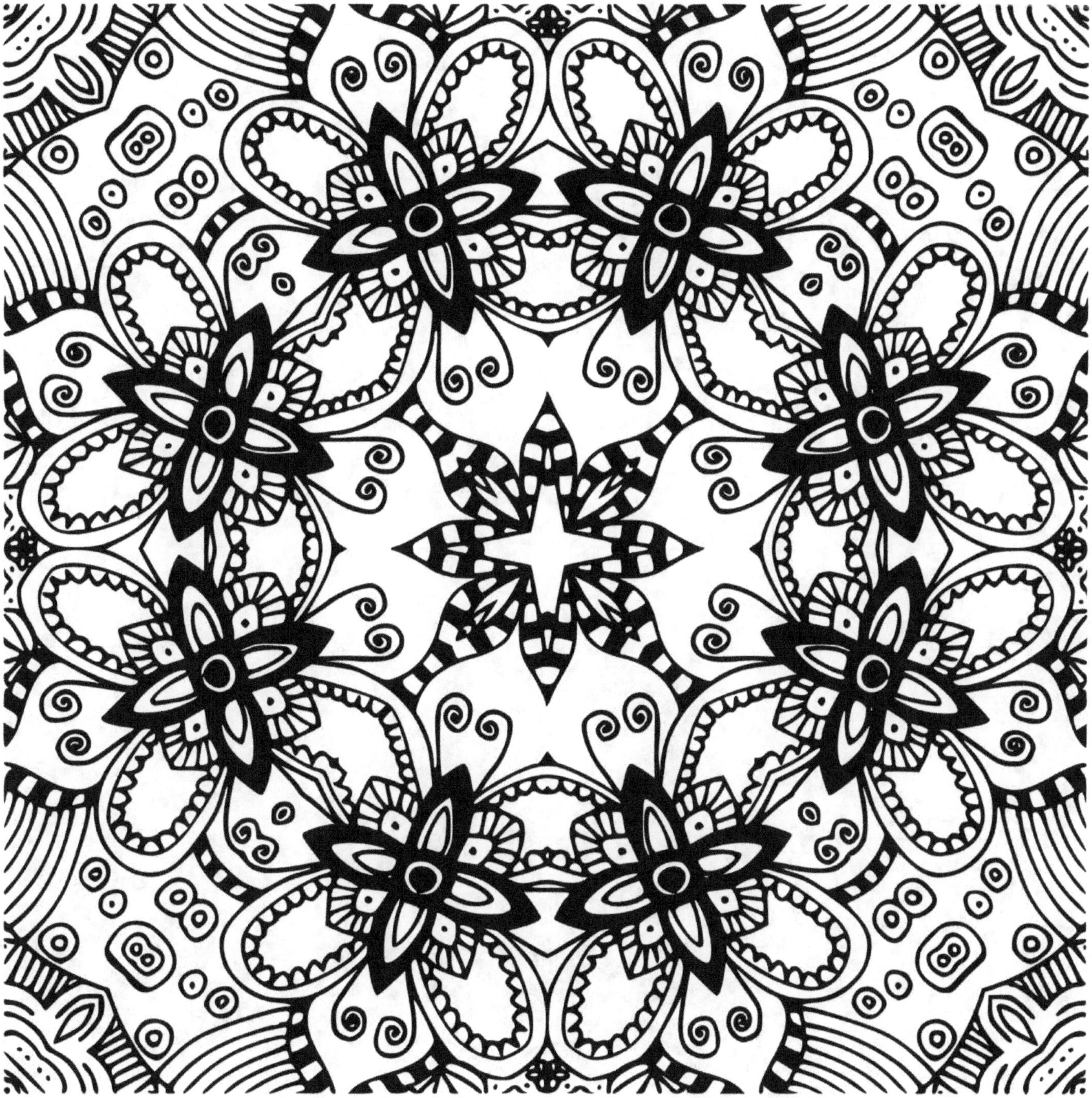

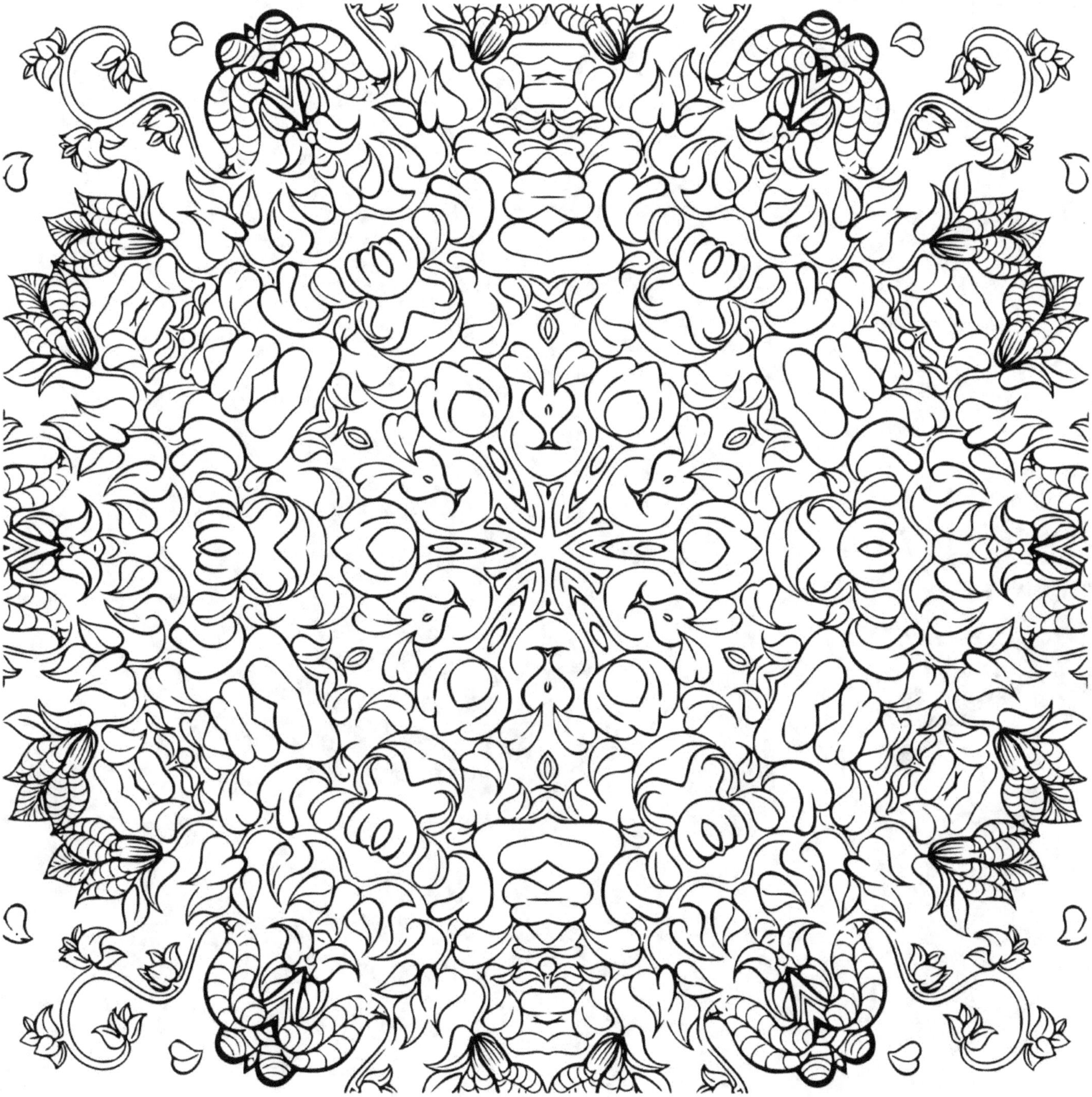

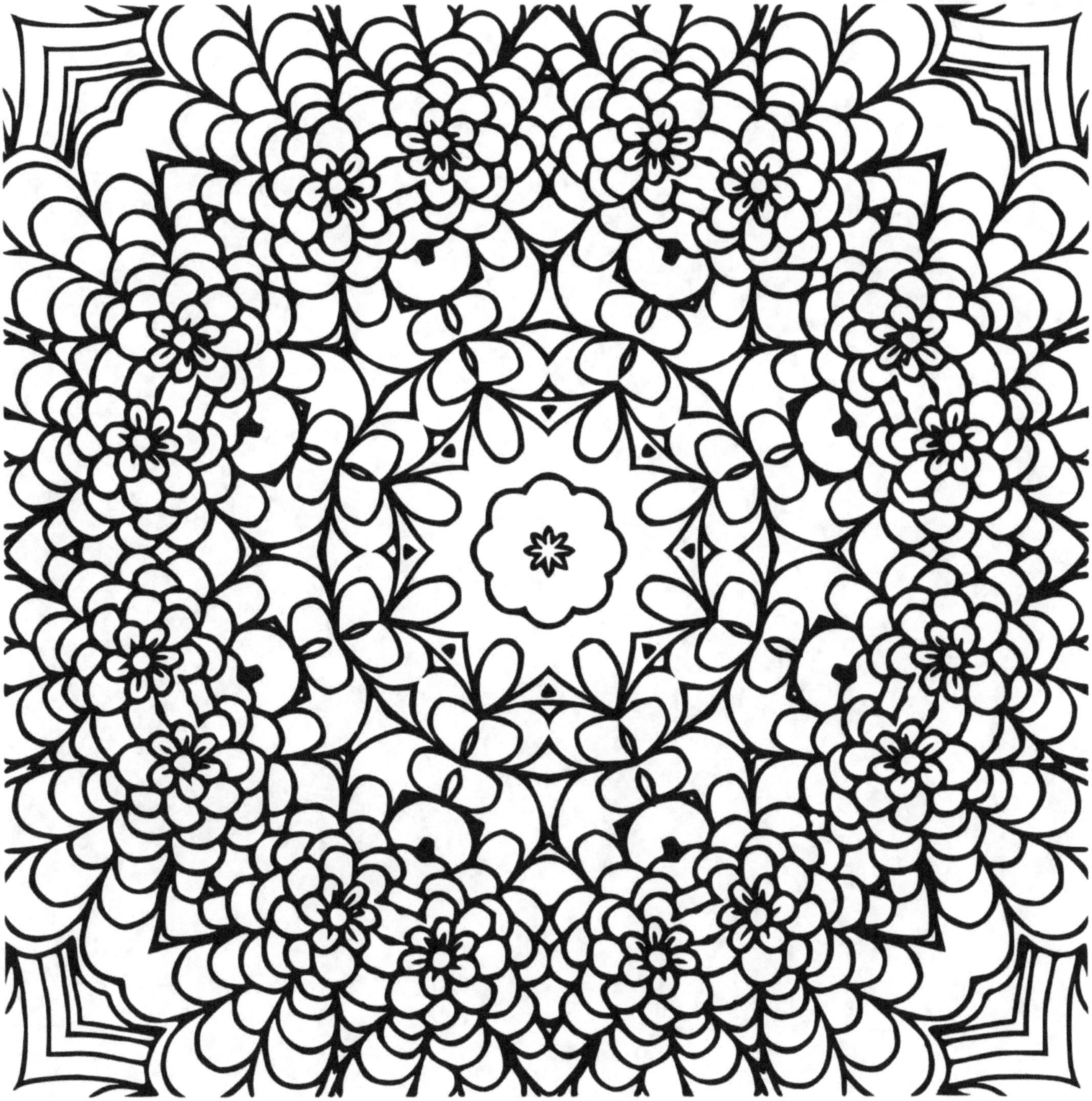

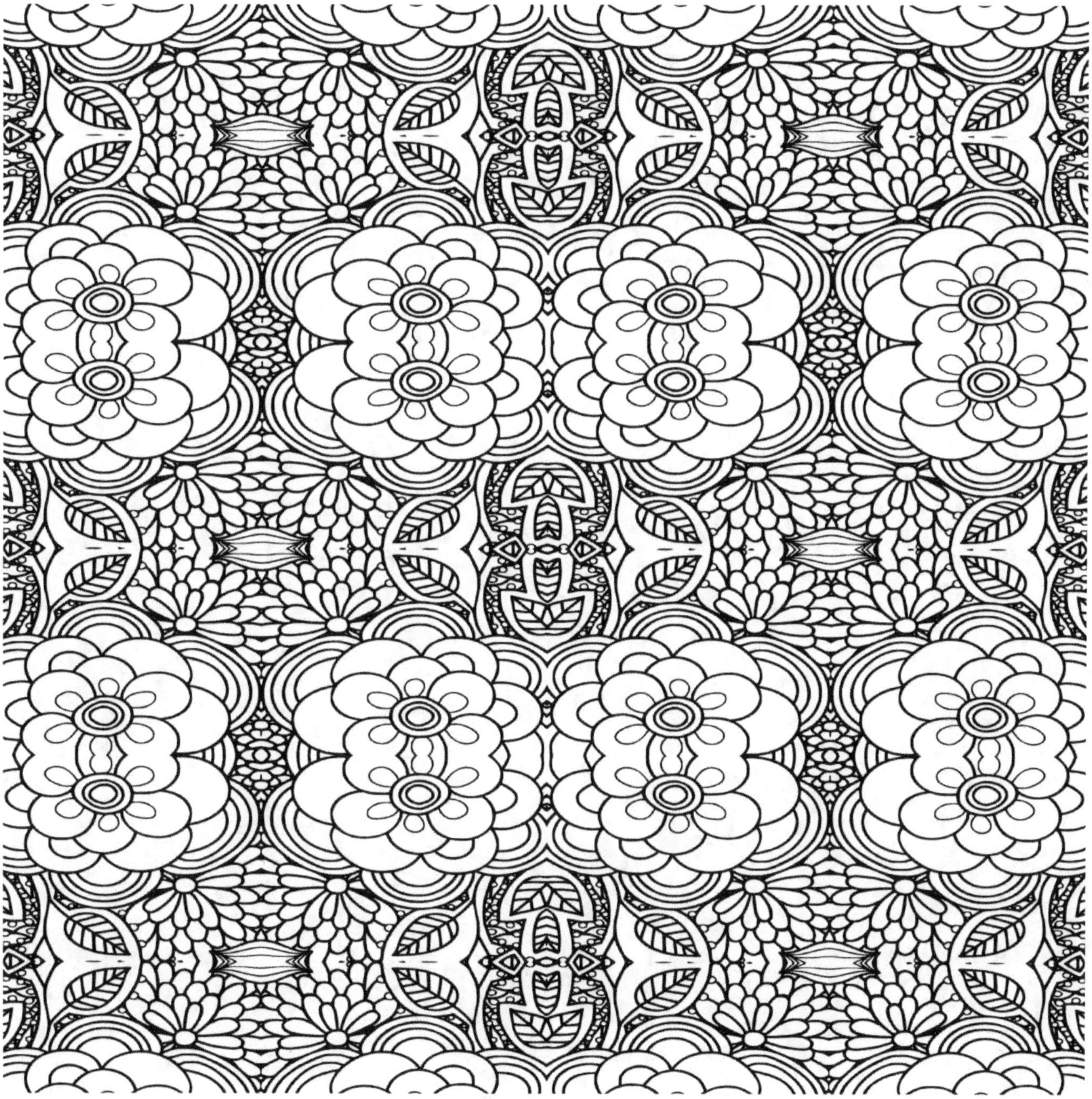

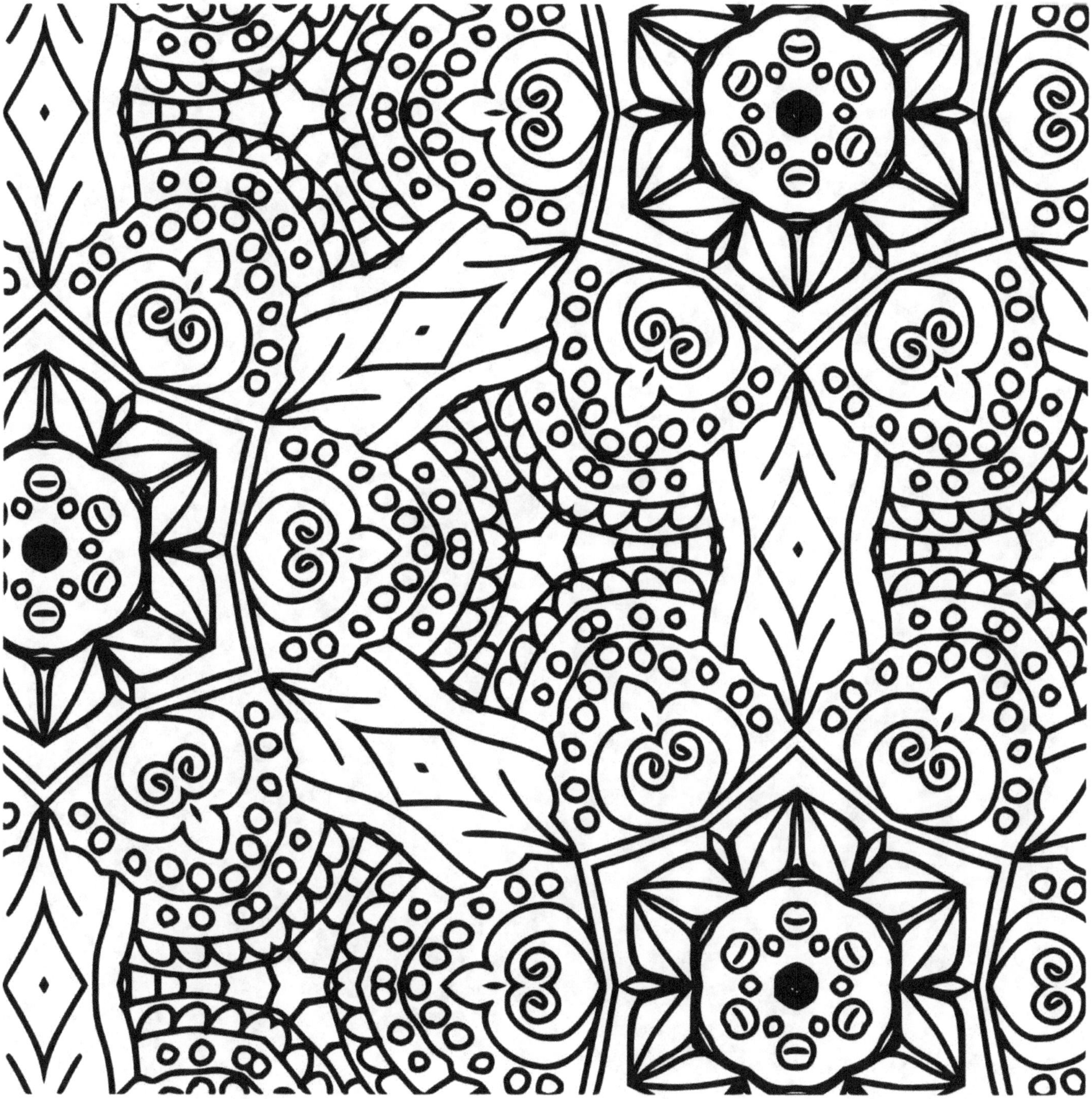

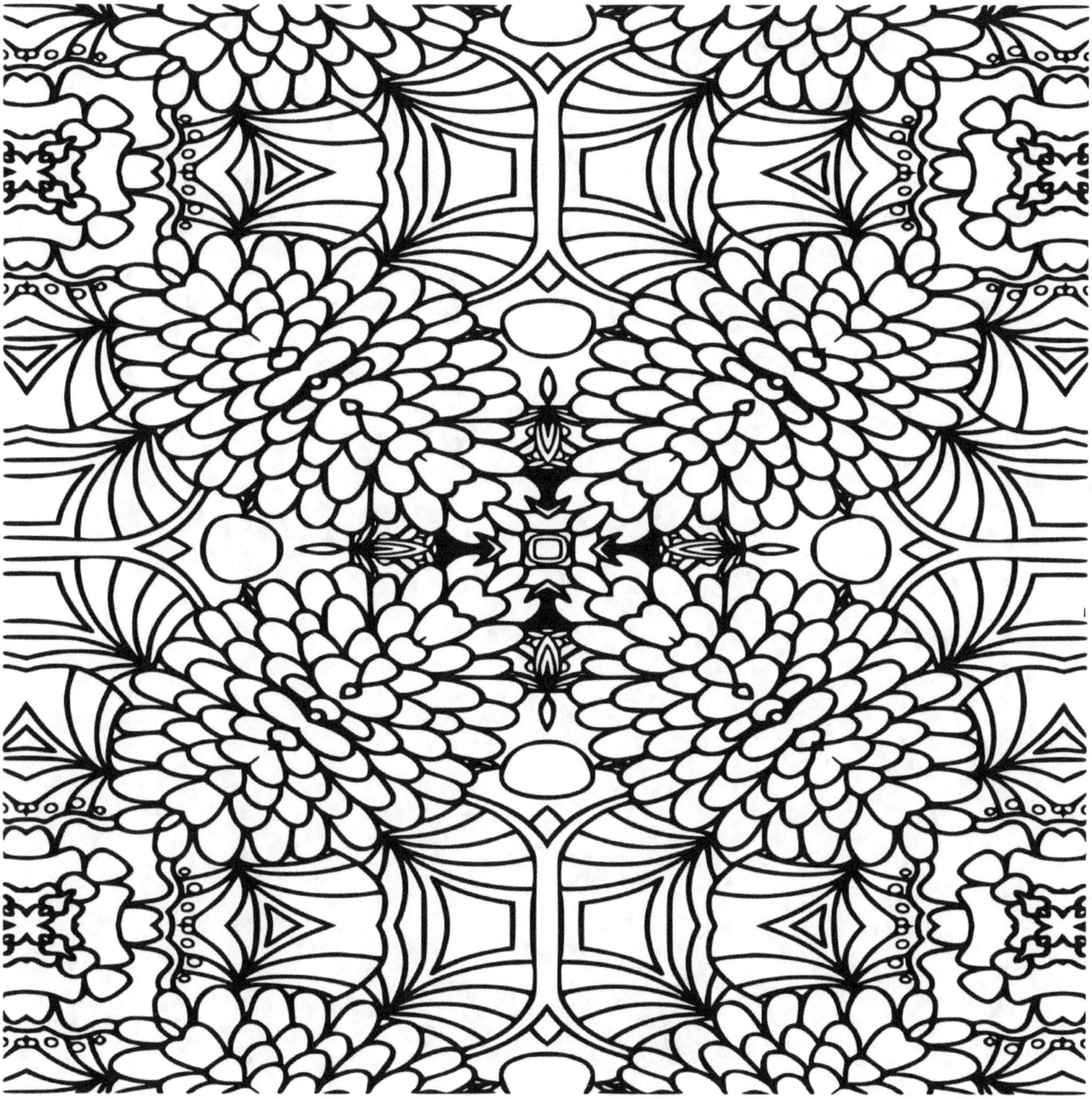

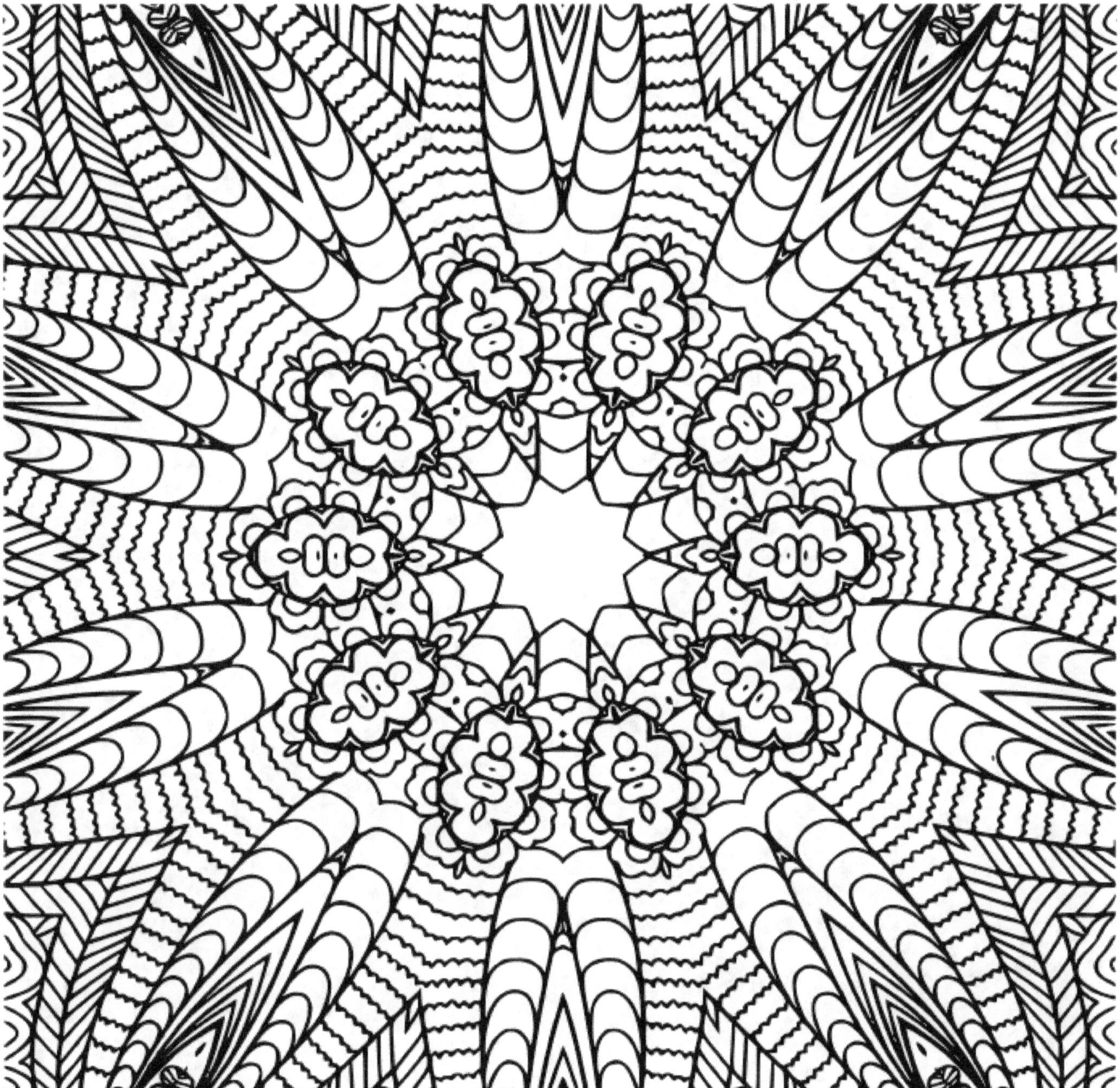

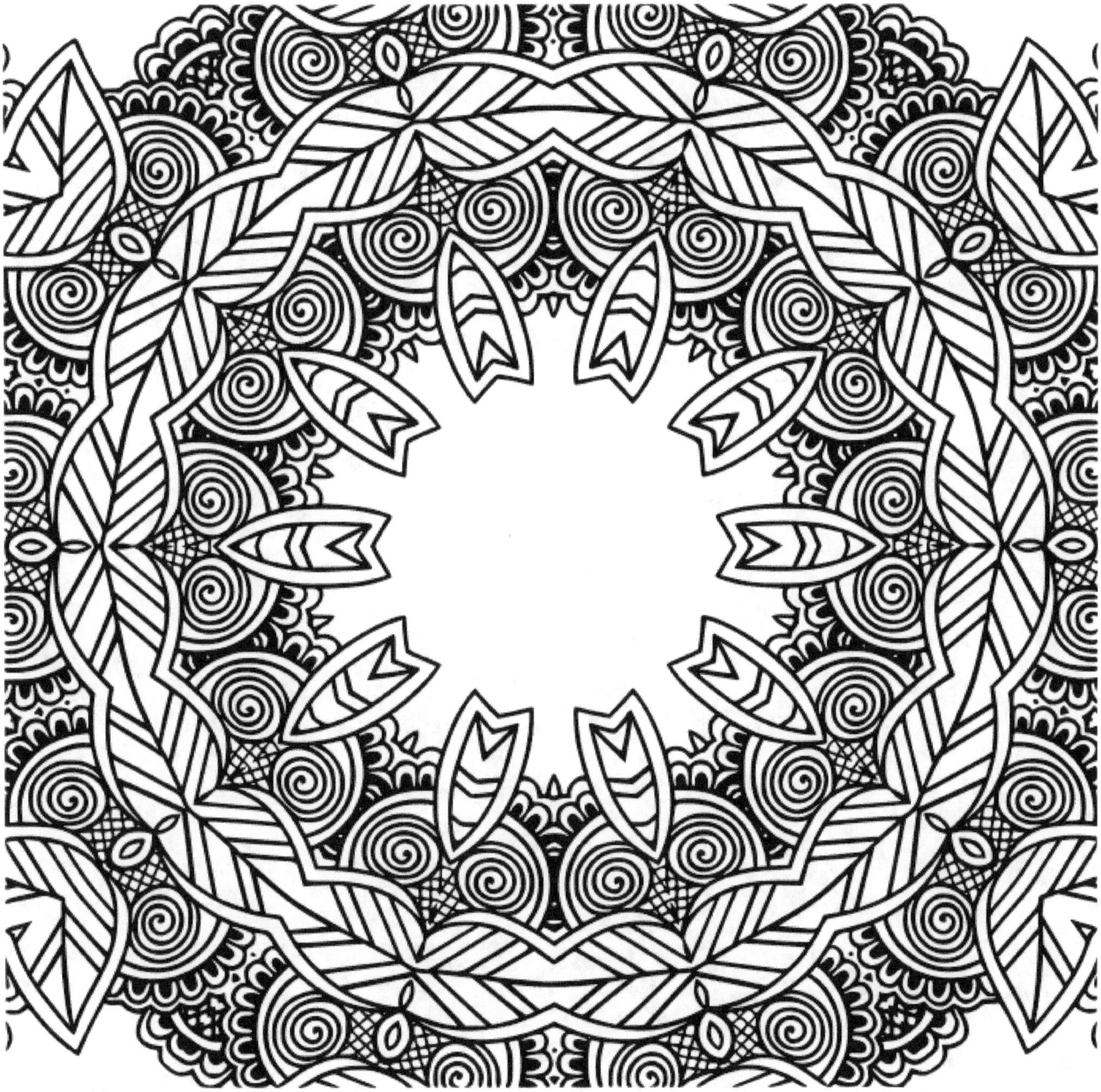

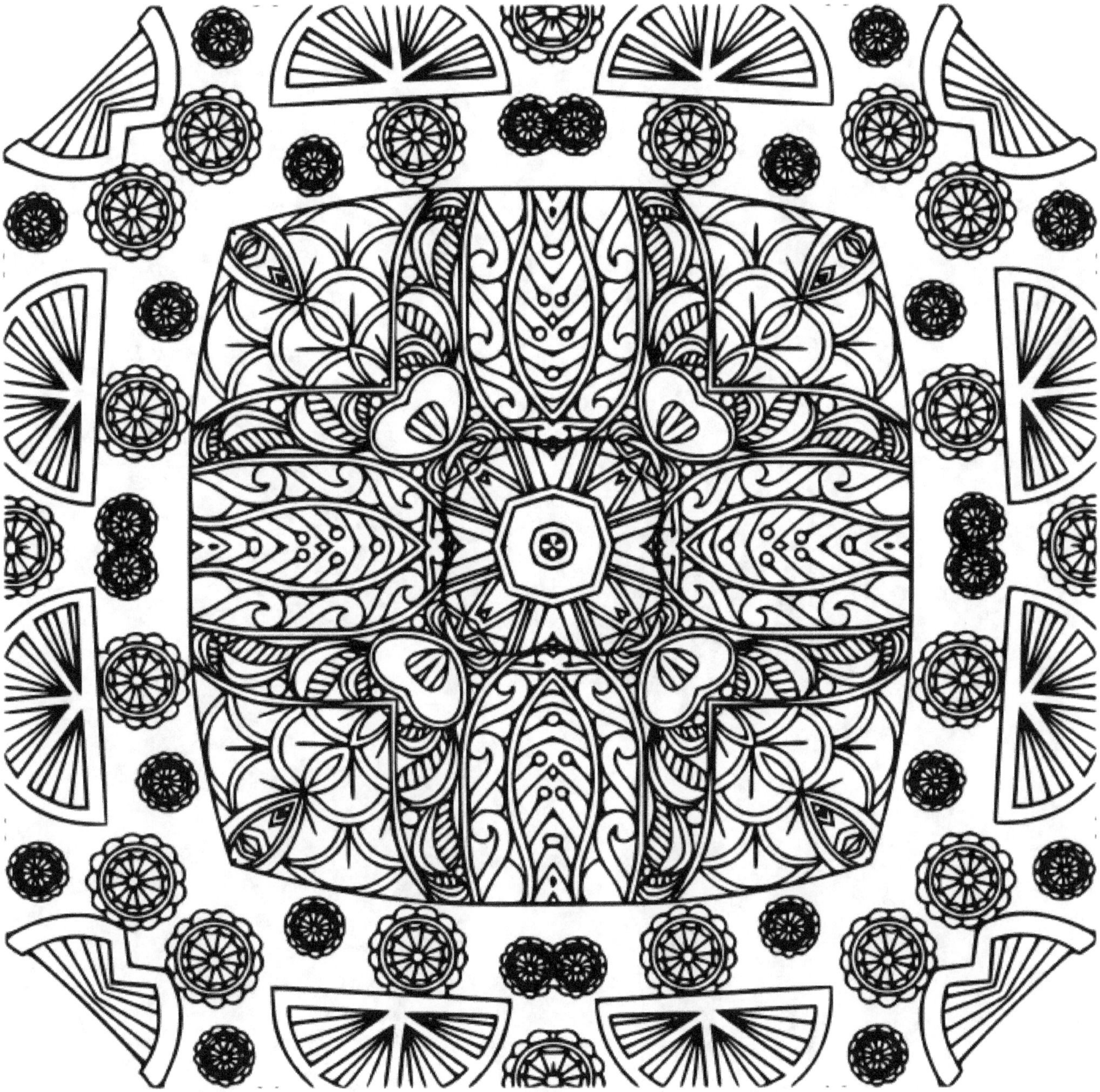

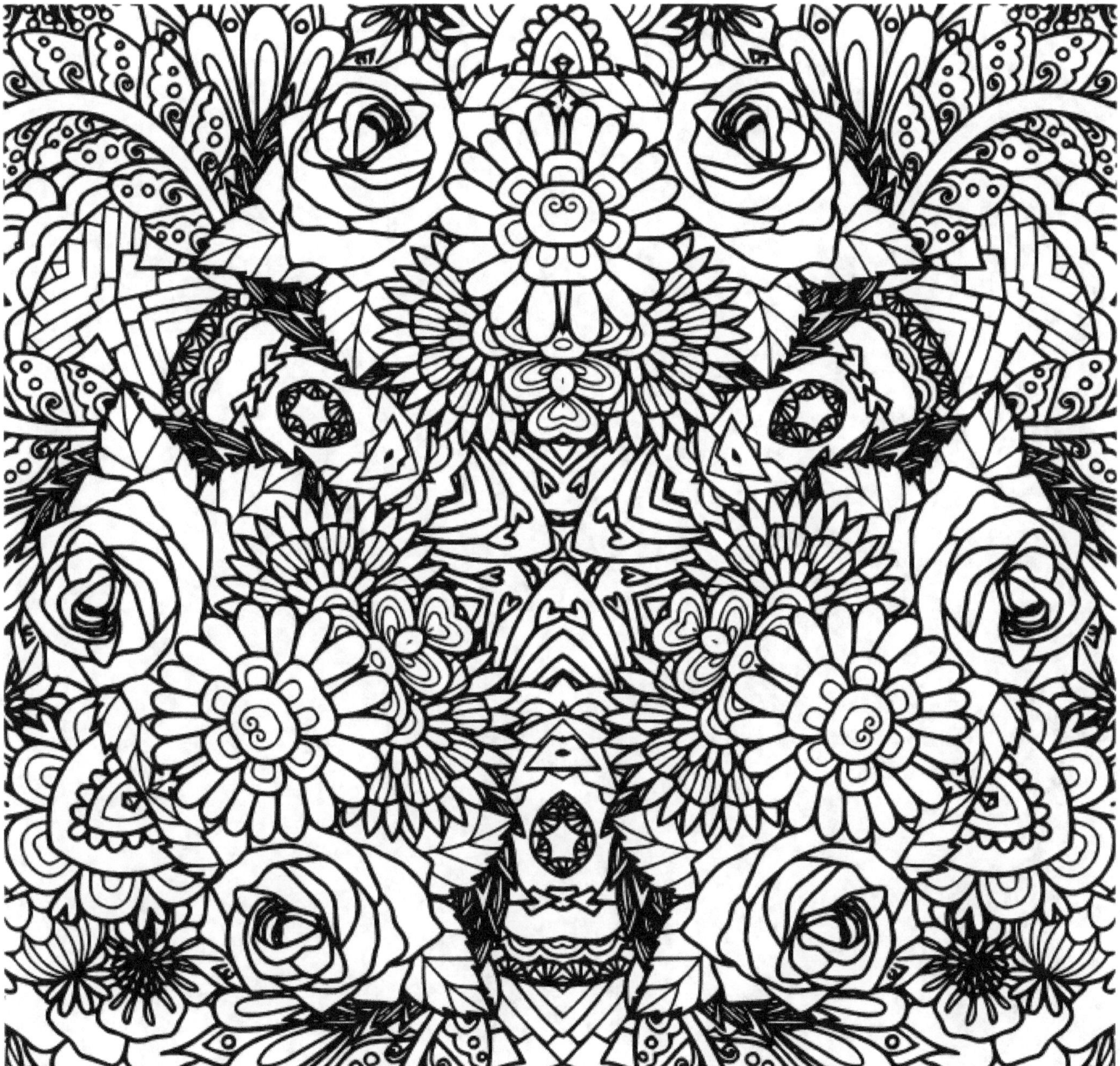

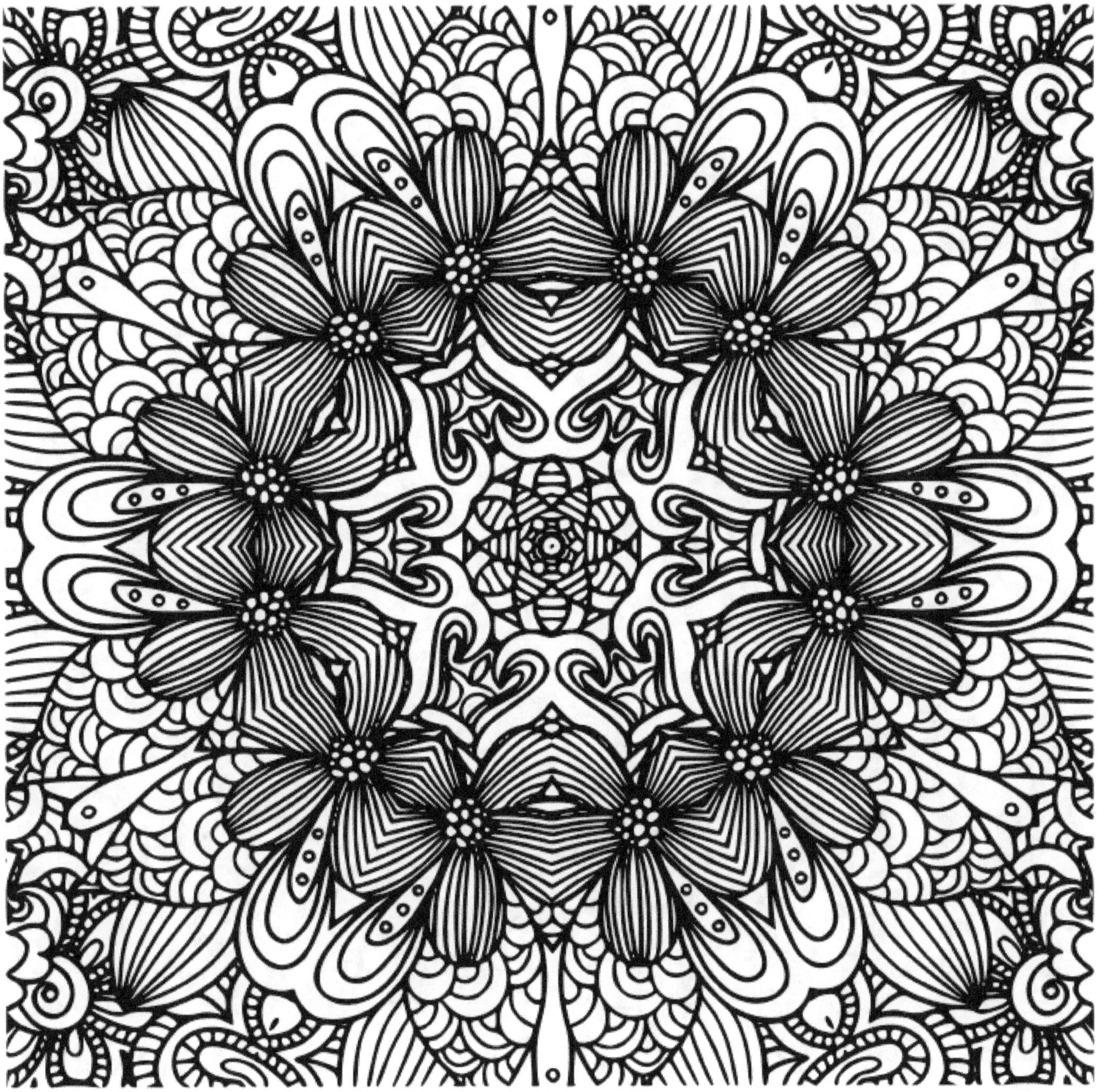

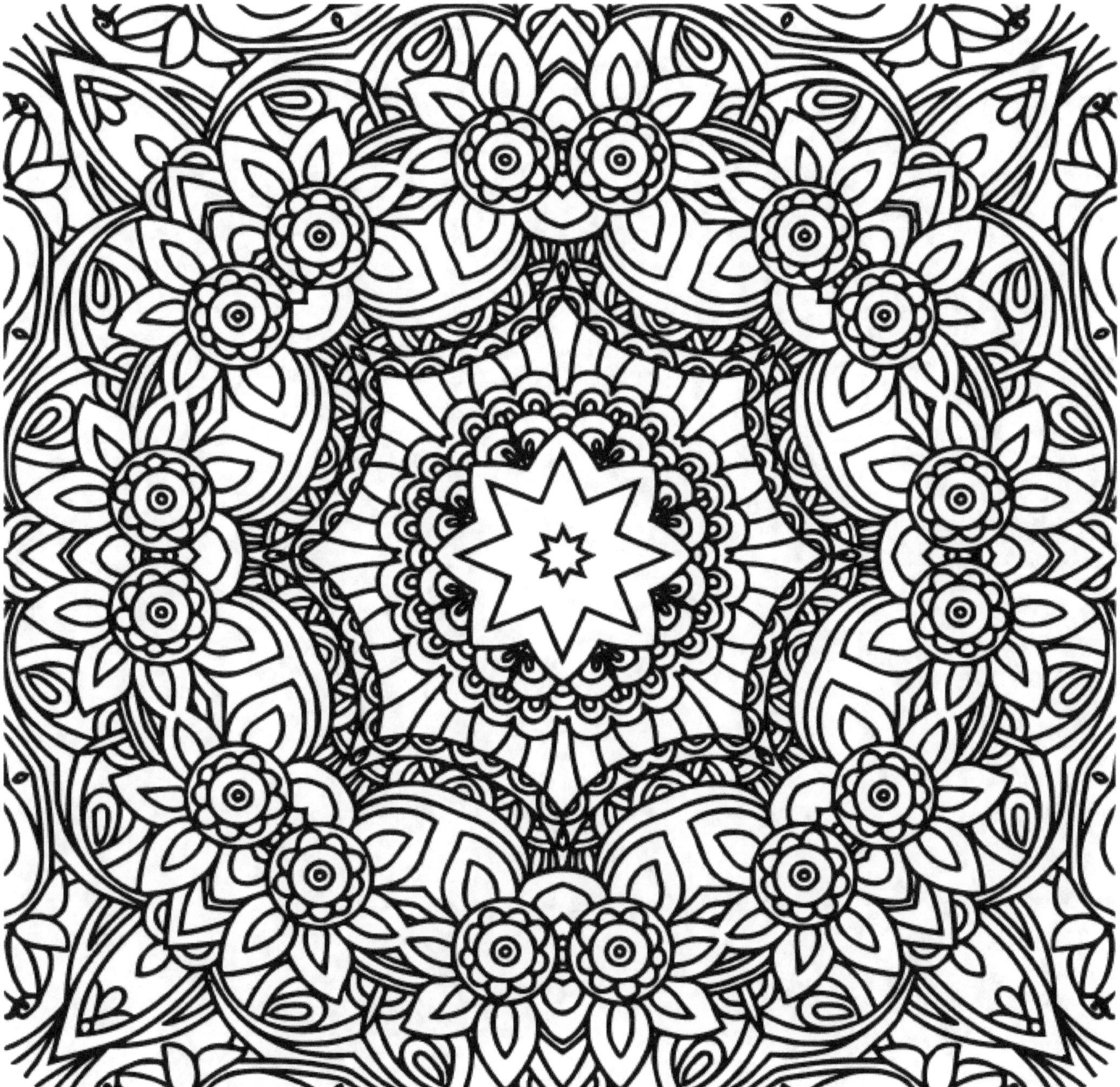

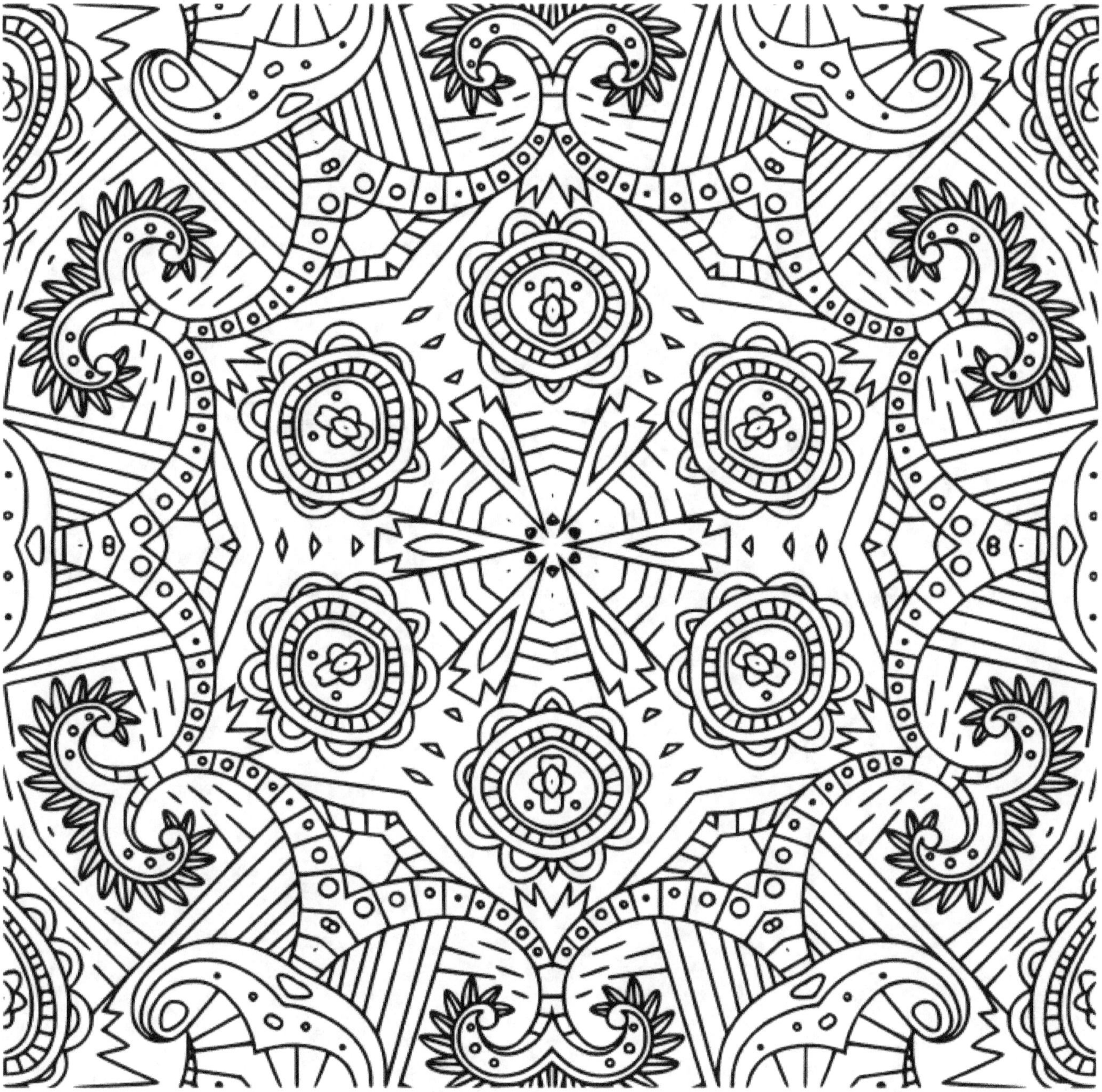

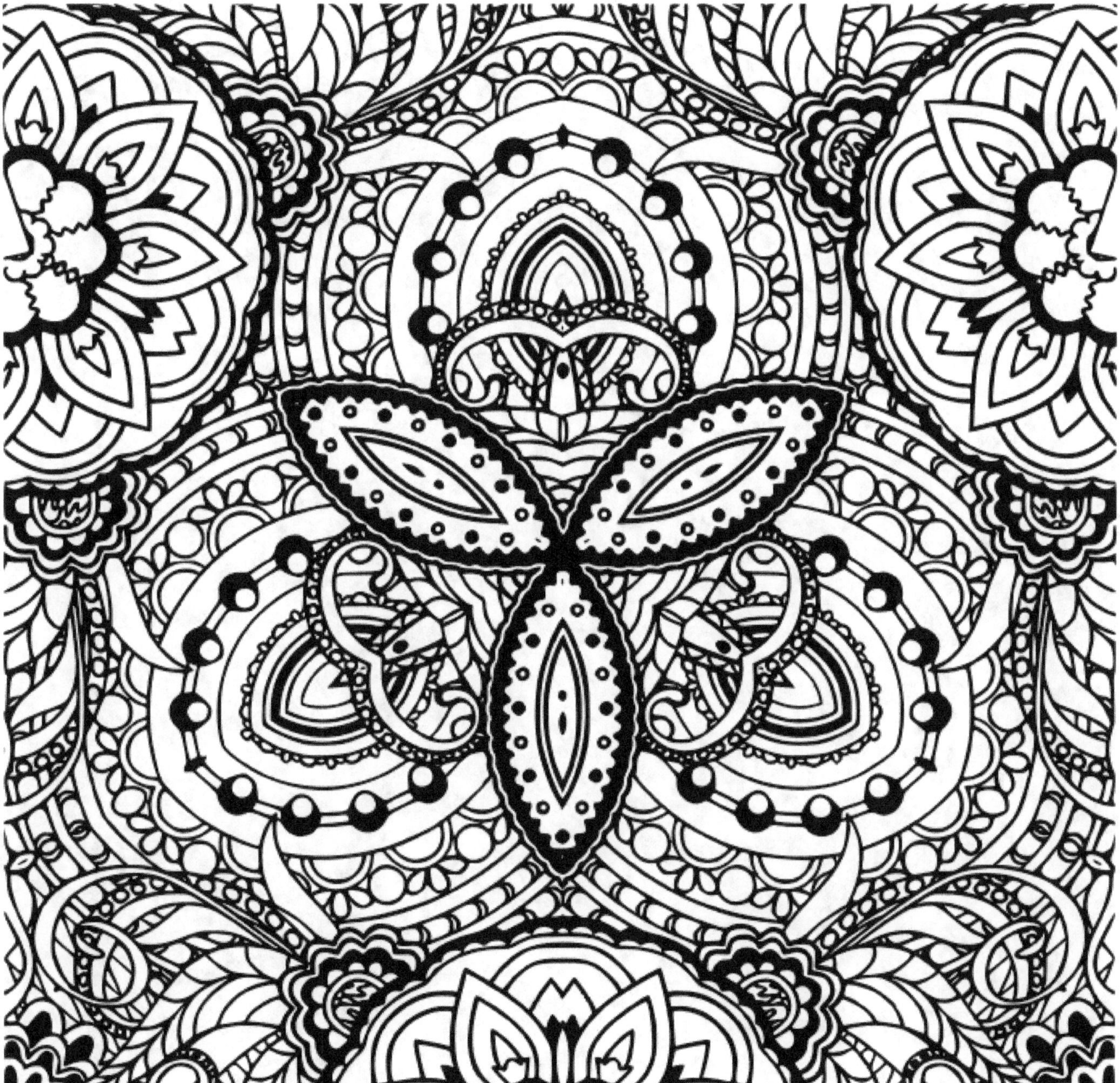

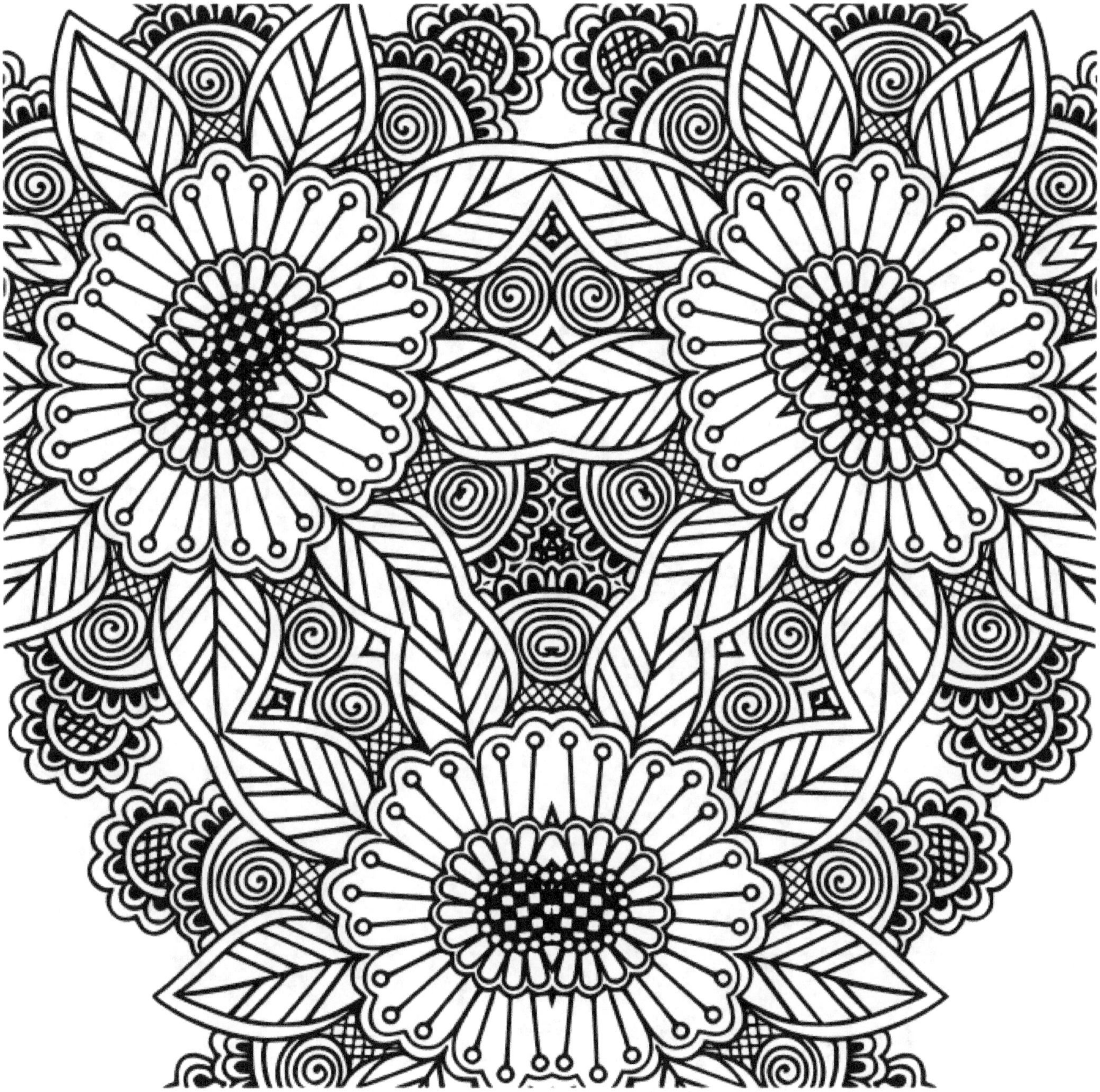

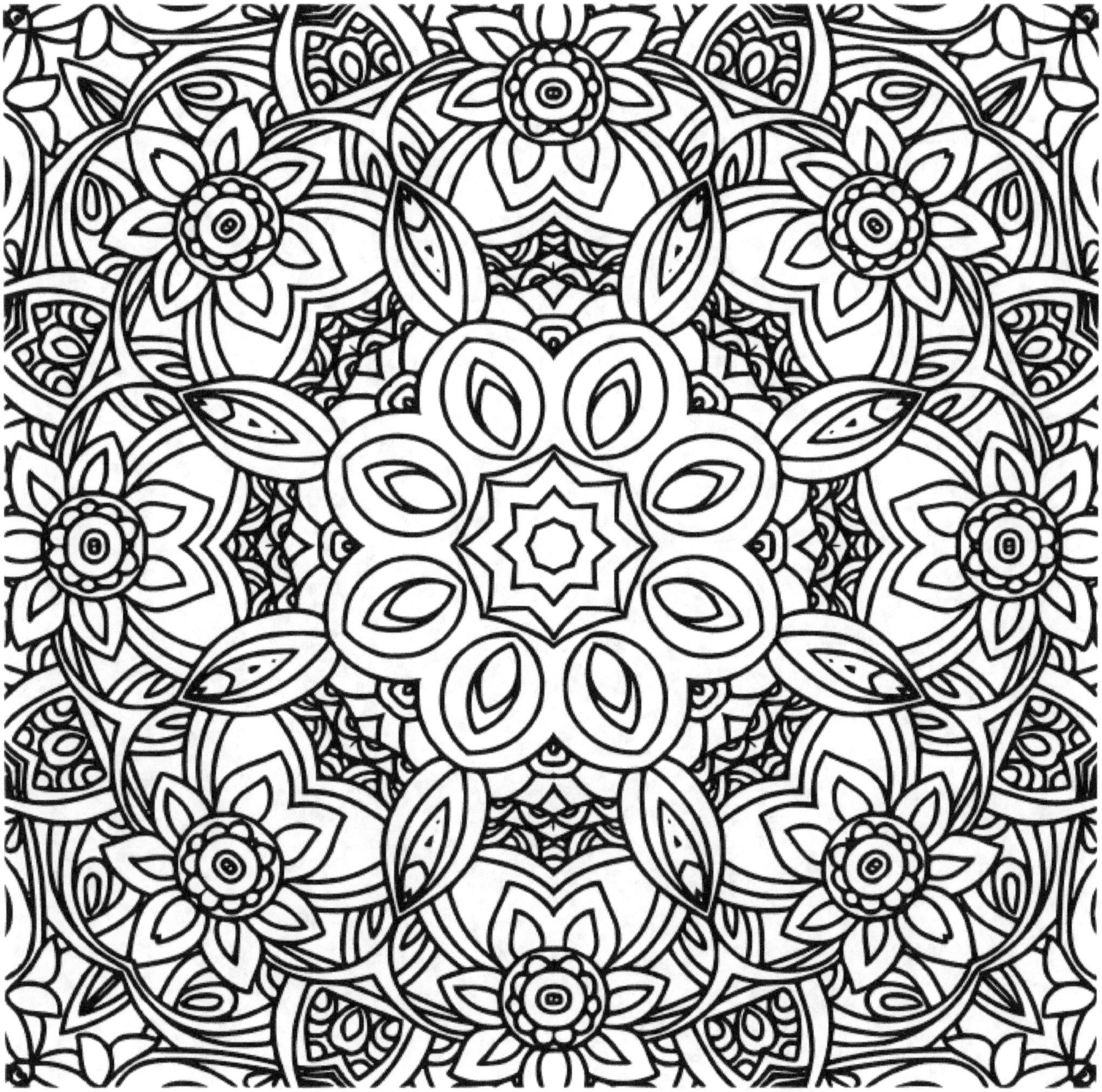

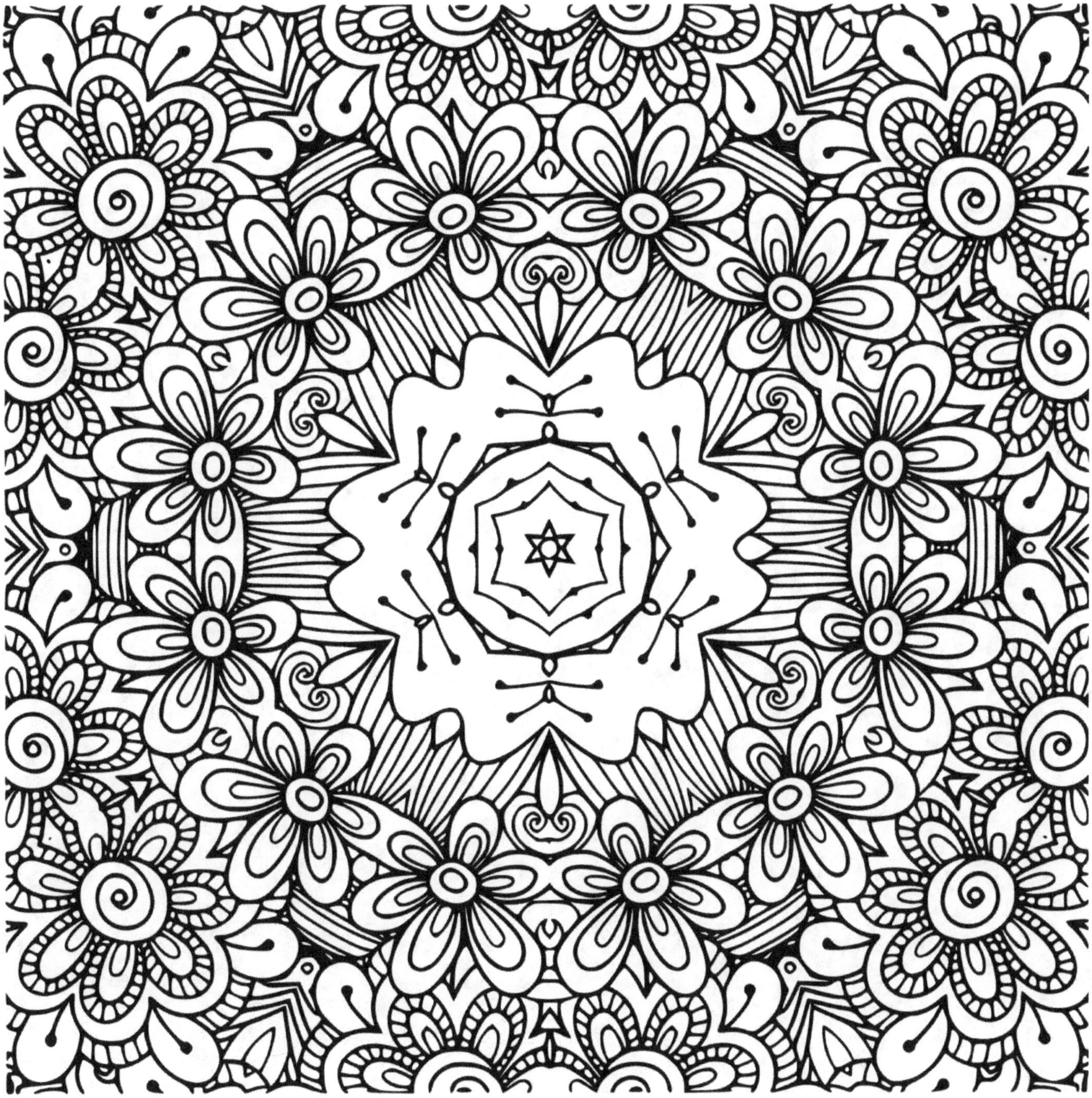

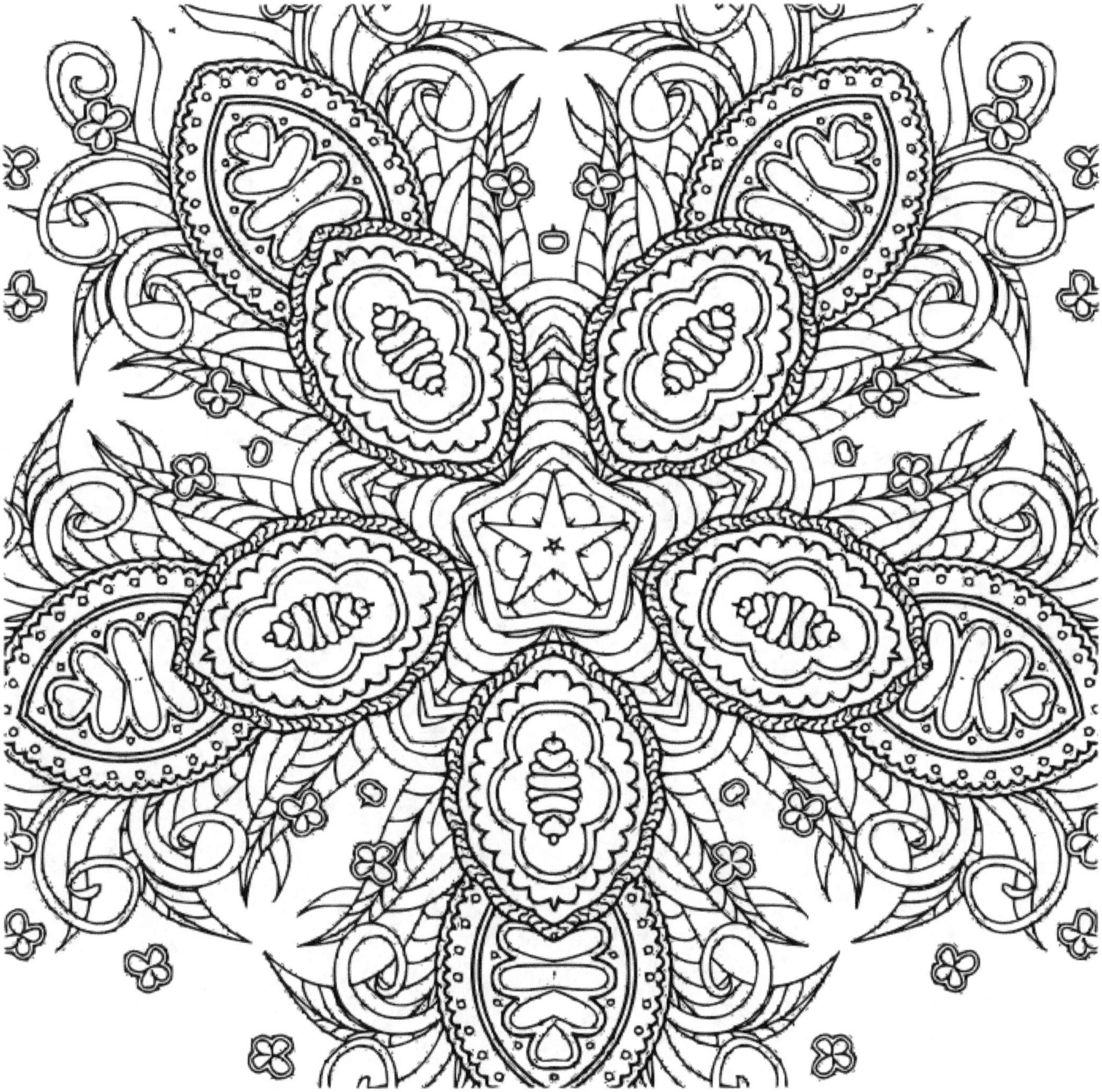

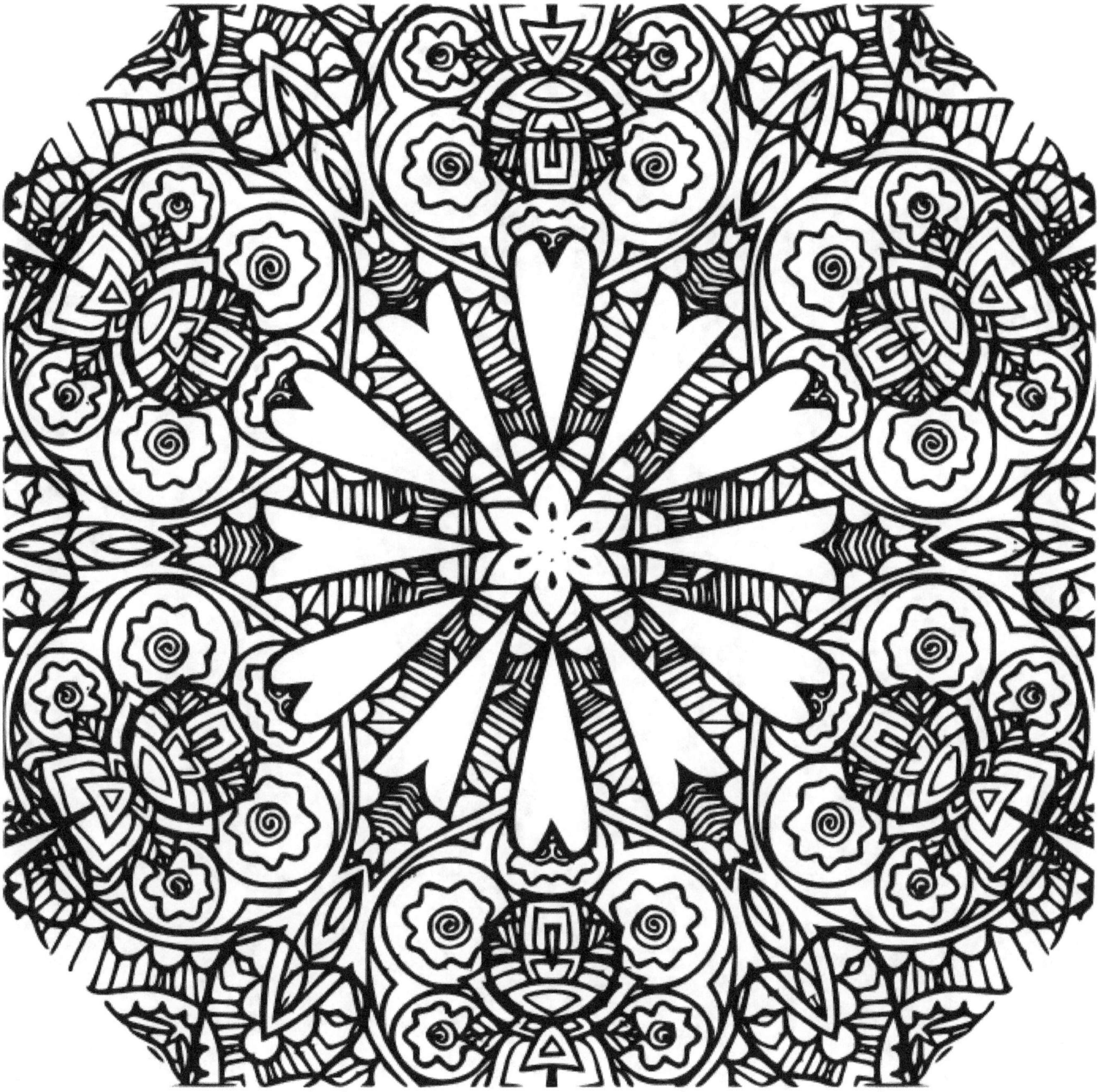

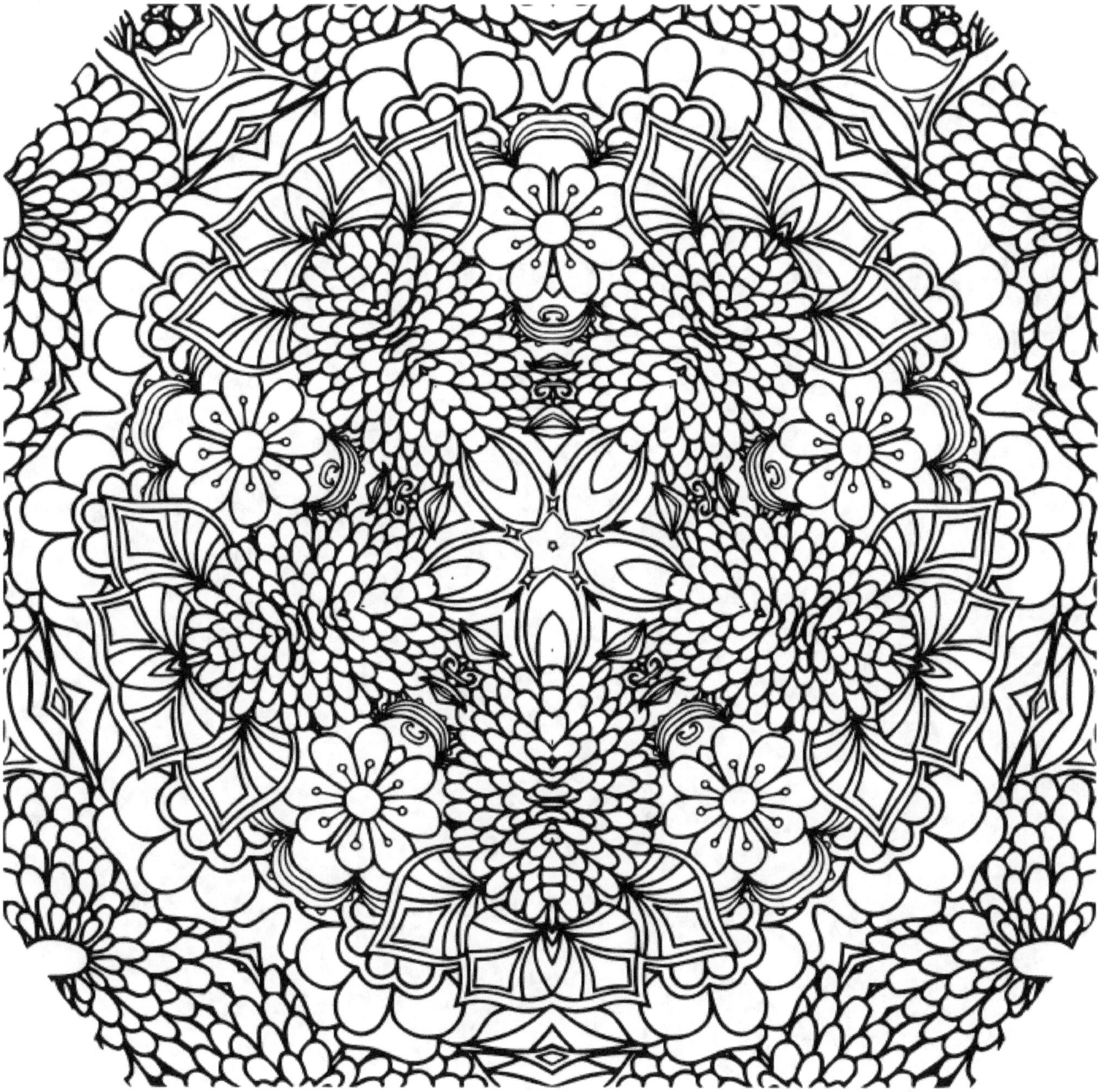

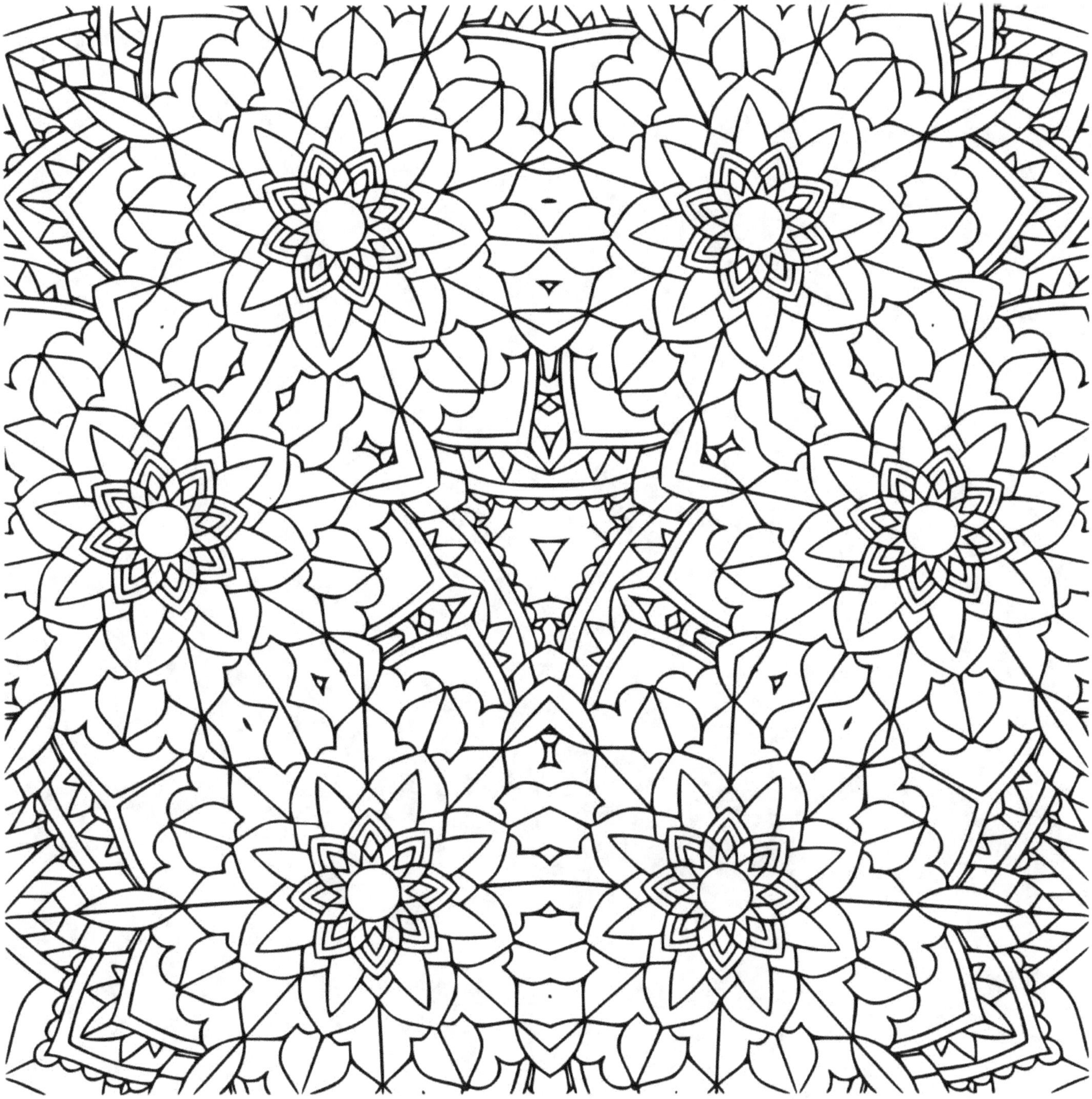

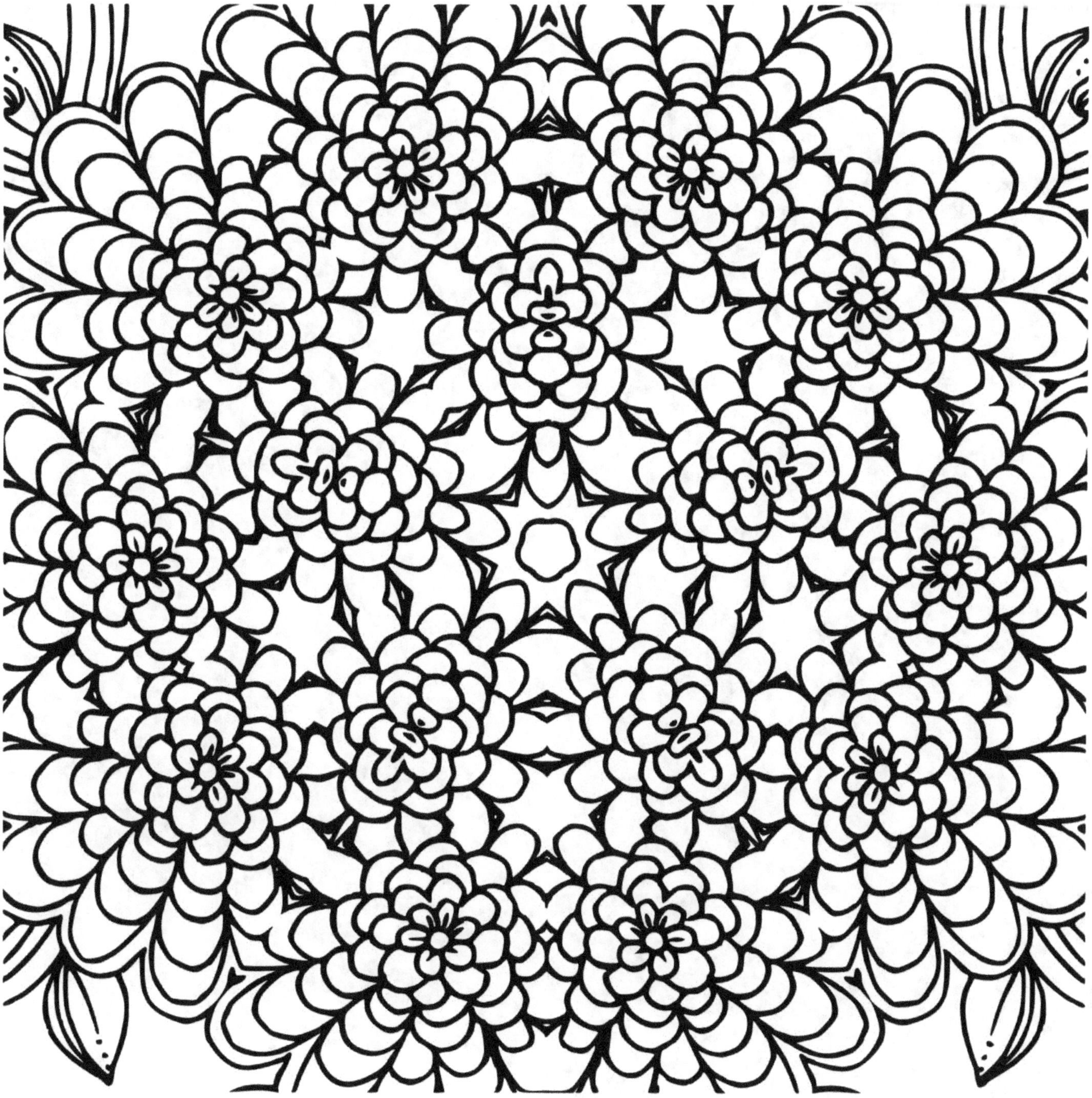

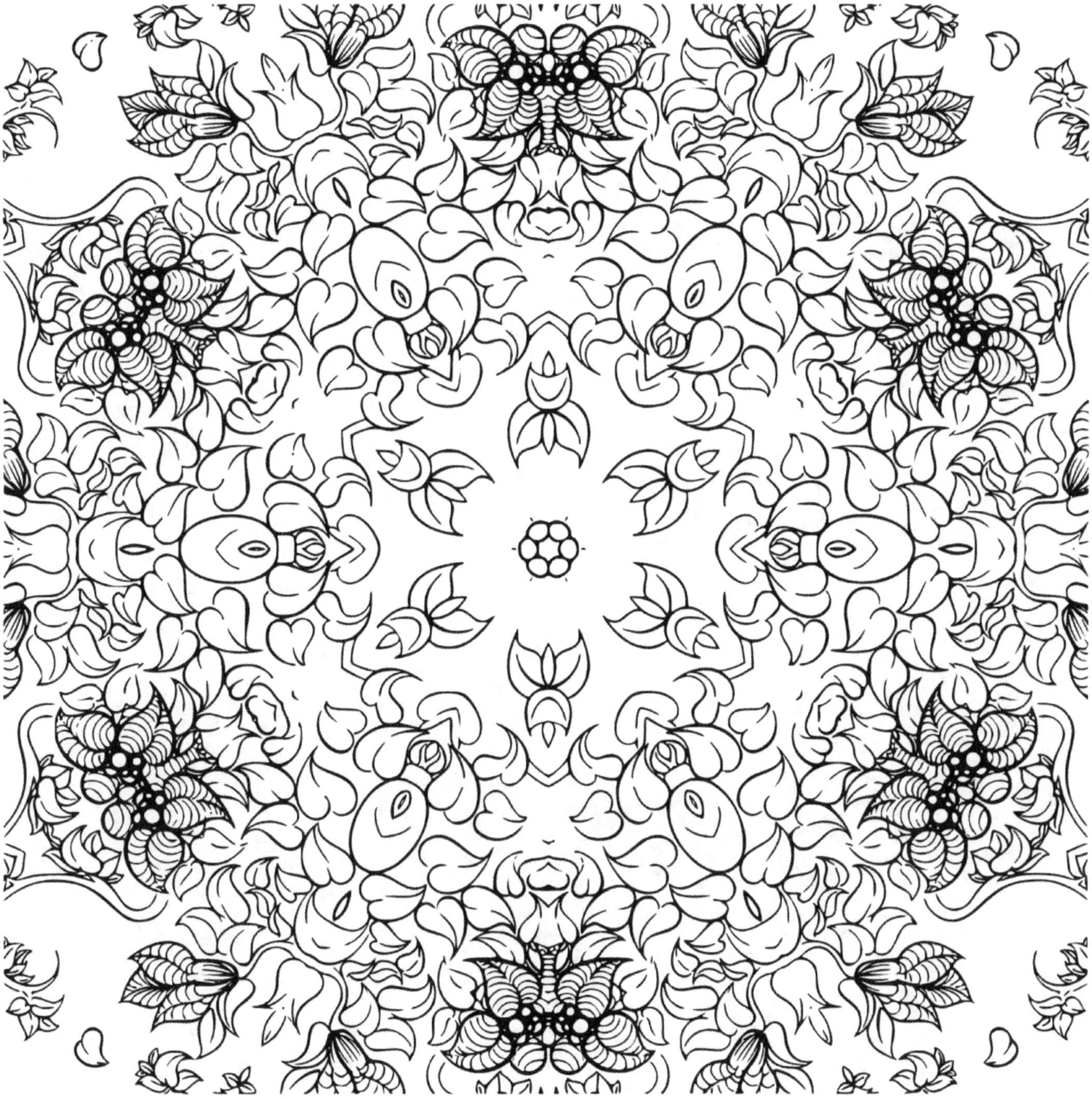

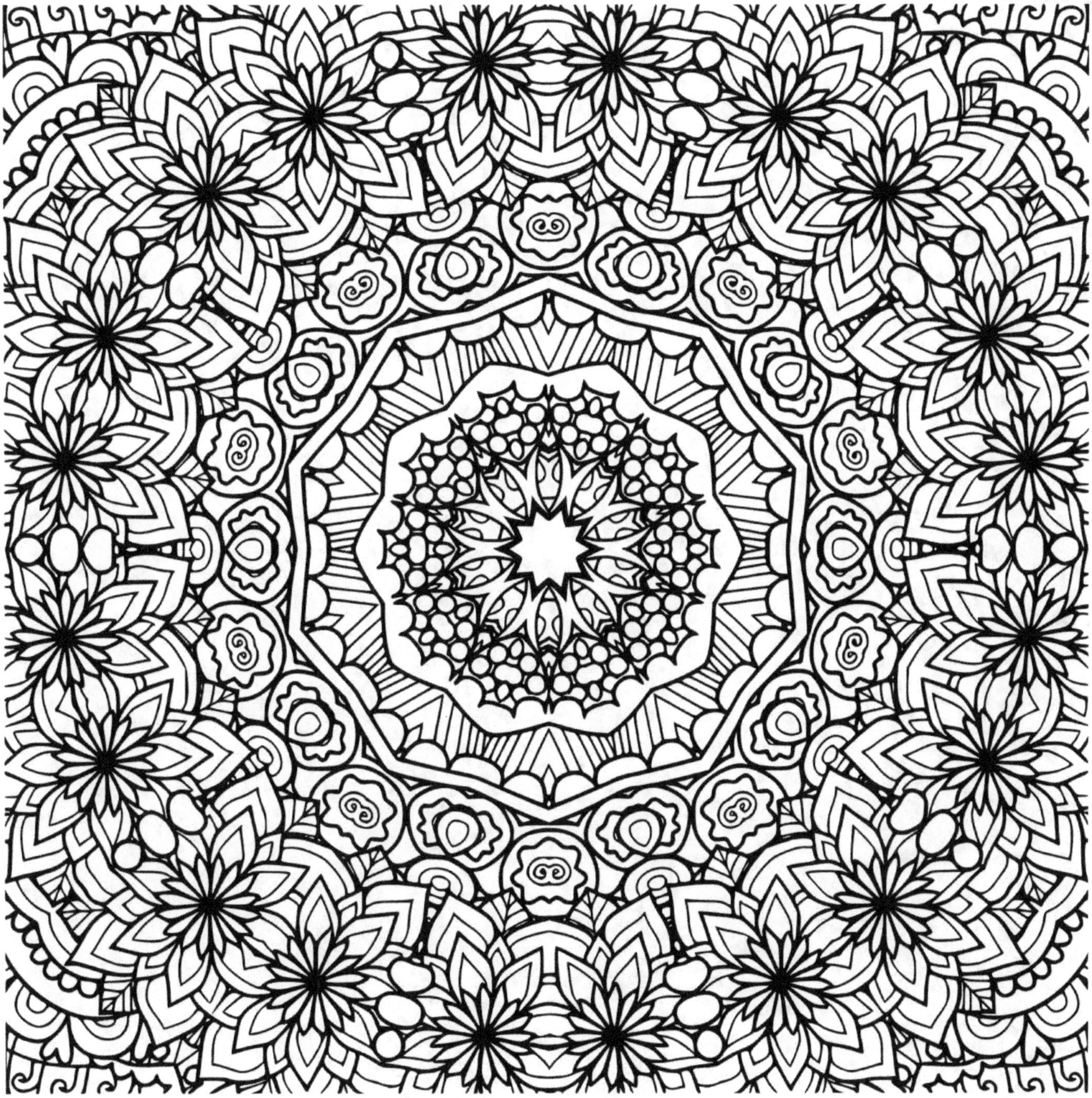

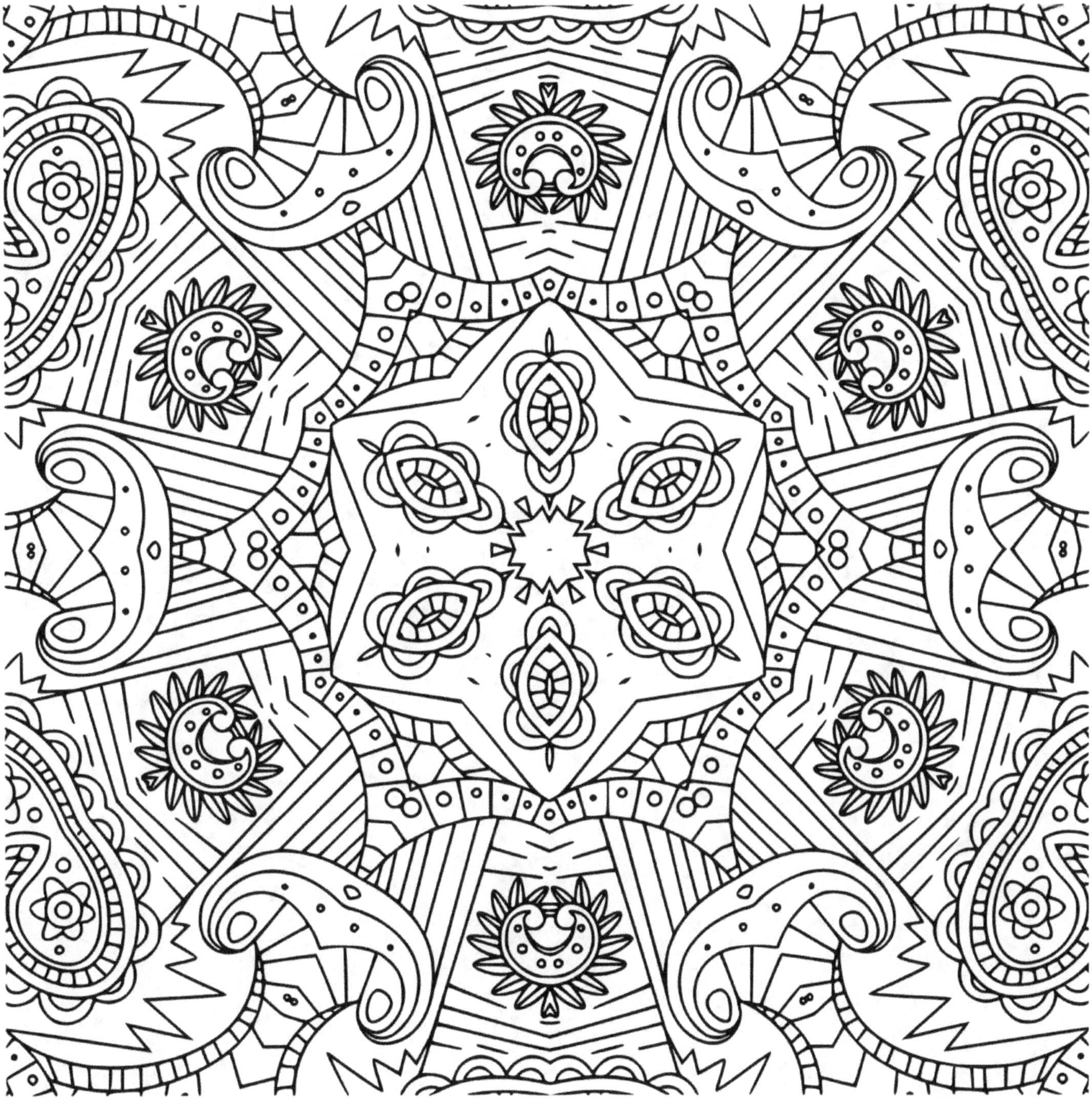

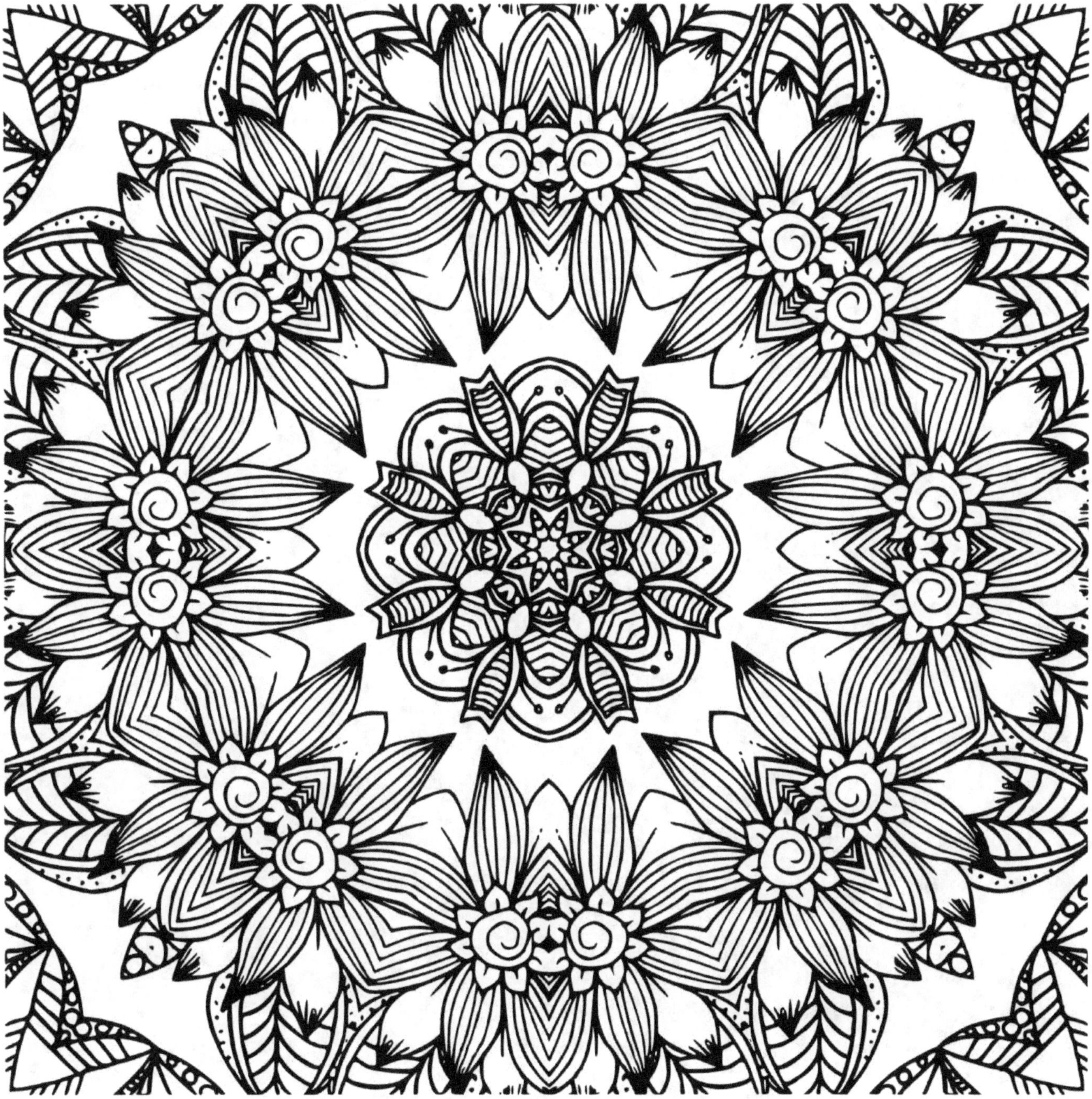

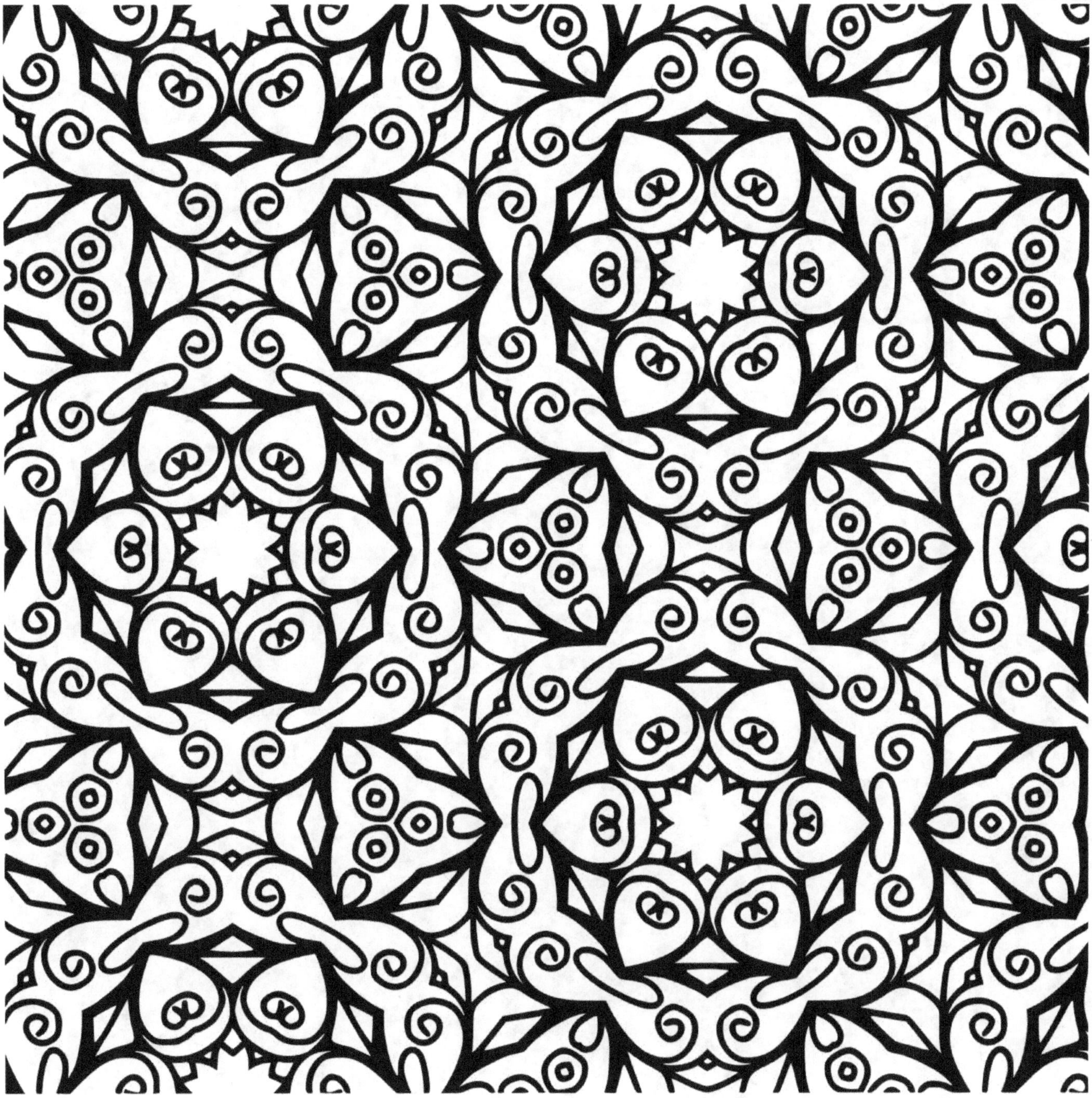

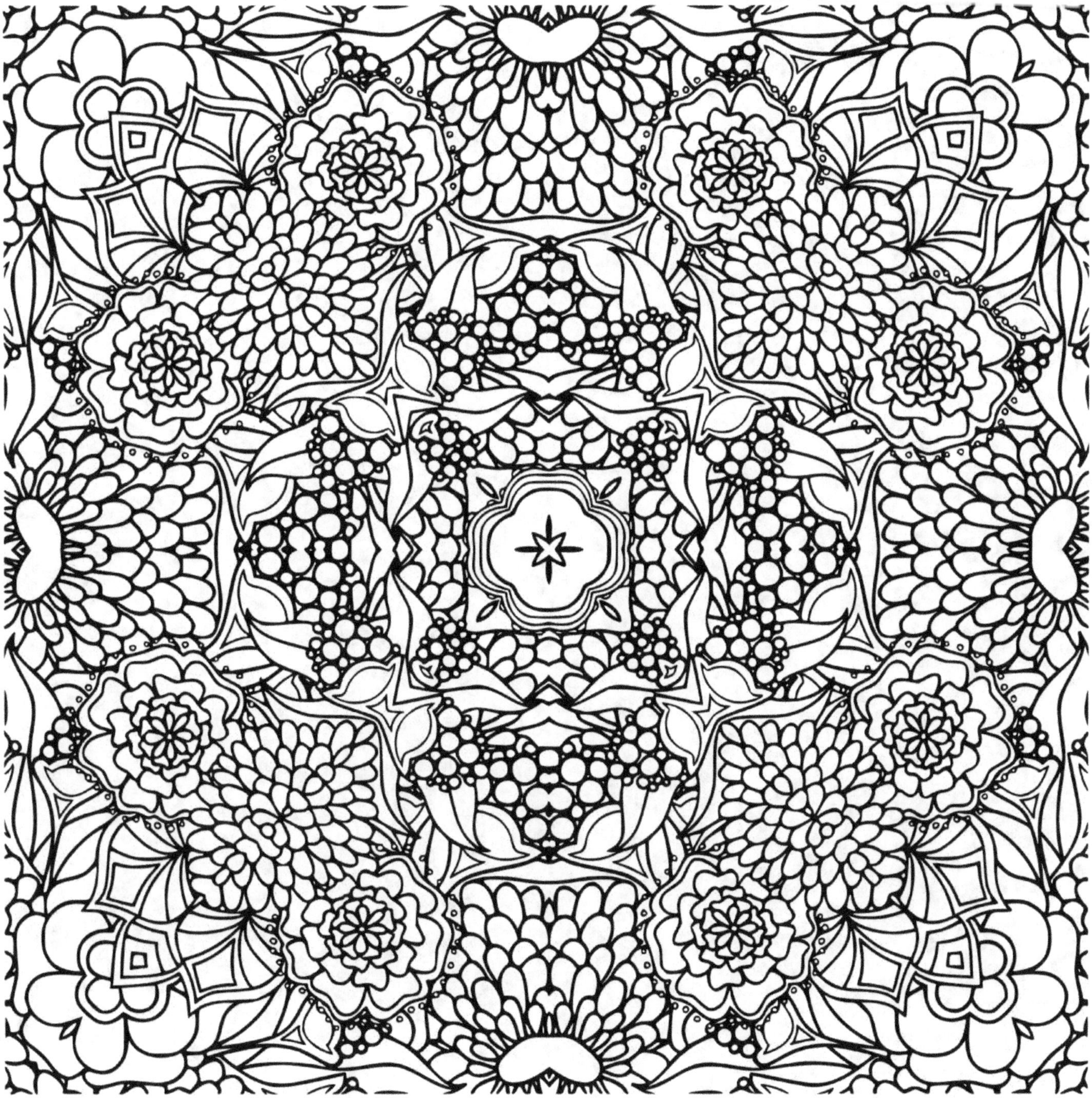

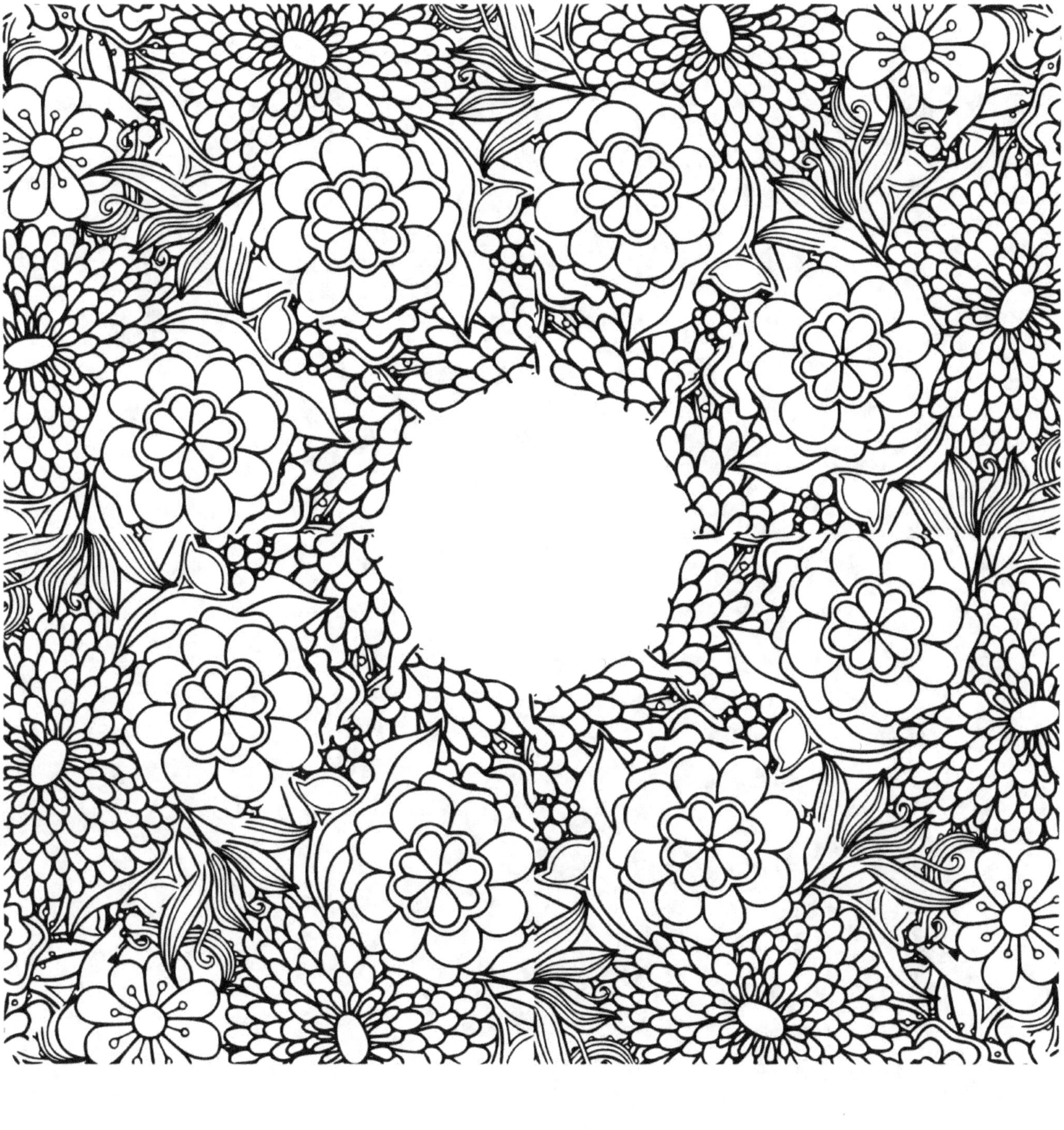

www.ingramcontent.com/pod-product-compliance
Lightning Source LLC
Chambersburg PA
CBHW080553220526
45466CB00010B/3136
* 9 7 9 8 5 5 1 9 0 7 0 1 5 *